W9-BSJ-651

17.96

HOME REPAIR AND IMPROVEMENT

INSULATING AND WEATHERPROOFING

TIME® LIFE BOOKS

OTHER PUBLICATIONS:

DO IT YOURSELF
The Time-Life Complete Gardener
Home Repair and Improvement
The Art of Woodworking
Fix It Yourself

COOKING
Weight Watchers® Smart Choice Recipe Collection
Great Taste/Low Fat
Williams-Sonoma Kitchen Library

HISTORY
The American Story
Voices of the Civil War
The American Indians
Lost Civilizations
Mysteries of the Unknown
Time Frame
The Civil War
Cultural Atlas

TIME-LIFE KIDS
Family Time Bible Stories
Library of First Questions and Answers
A Child's First Library of Learning
I Love Math
Nature Company Discoveries
Understanding Science & Nature

SCIENCE/NATURE
Voyage Through the Universe

For information on and a full description
of any of the Time-Life Books series listed above,
please call 1-800-621-7026 or write:

Reader Information
Time-Life Customer Service
P.O. Box C-32068
Richmond Virginia 23261-2068

CONTENTS

1 Keeping a House Snug and Tight

Weatherproofing a home is a matter of establishing priorities. It's best to focus your efforts where they will do the most good—and save you the most money. The first areas to address are leaky doors and windows. For most homes, this means finding and filling small openings all over the house. A few dollars spent applying weather stripping and sealing gaps will be repaid many times over.

Sealing around an outdoor faucet →

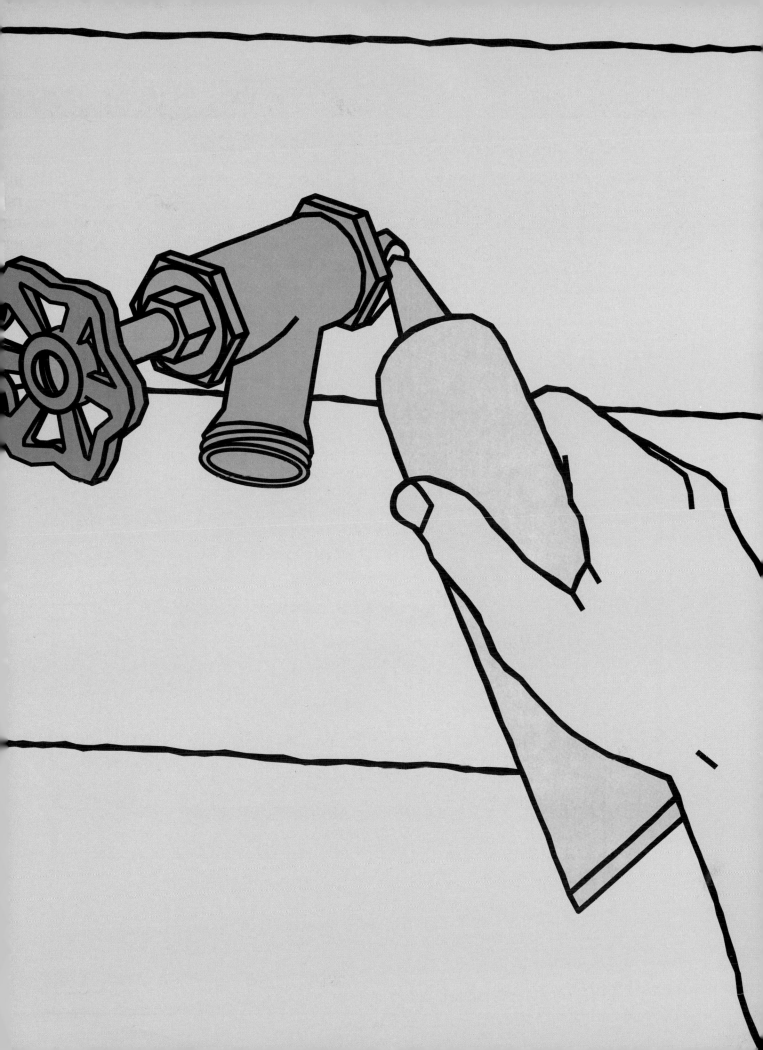

Blocking Drafts Around Windows

Gaps around doors and windows are the main causes of air leakage in most homes. Sealing these gaps with weather stripping can reduce heating and air-conditioning costs by as much as 30 percent.

Preparing Windows: Before applying stripping, make sure the windows work properly. Try scraping or sanding paint or dirt off the sashes and their channels.

A Range of Solutions: One of the simplest ways to block window drafts in winter is with an inexpensive window insulator kit *(pages 12-13)*. A plastic membrane is hung over the window and secured with double-faced tape. It can then be shrunk, forming a nearly invisible seal.

More permanent and versatile products include metal, plastic, rubber, and vinyl weather stripping *(below)*. For double-hung and sliding windows, spring-metal or vinyl flanges work well. Invisible when the window is shut, these products are secured along only one edge; the other edge springs out to block leaks. Tubular gaskets seal better than spring strips, but are not as durable. Adhesive-backed foam tapes are a good choice for casement windows.

 TOOLS

Tape measure
Hammer
Nail set
Utility knife
Screwdriver
Tin snips
Blow-dryer

 **MATERIALS**

Tubular gaskets
Adhesive-backed
  foam stripping
Spring strips
Casement
  window gasket
Vinyl-to-metal
  adhesive
Window insulator kit

SAFETY TIPS

Protect your eyes with goggles when driving nails.

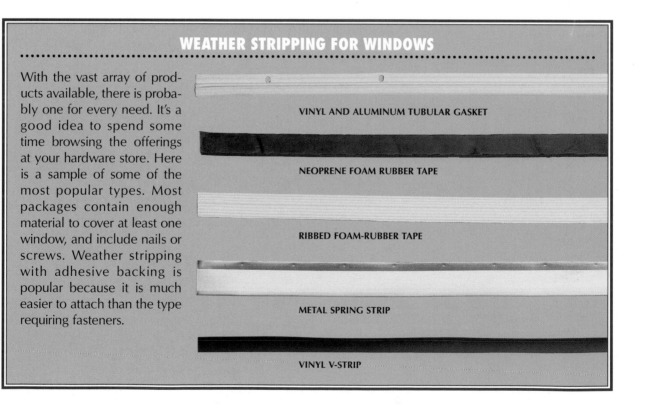

WEATHER STRIPPING FOR WINDOWS

With the vast array of products available, there is probably one for every need. It's a good idea to spend some time browsing the offerings at your hardware store. Here is a sample of some of the most popular types. Most packages contain enough material to cover at least one window, and include nails or screws. Weather stripping with adhesive backing is popular because it is much easier to attach than the type requiring fasteners.

VINYL AND ALUMINUM TUBULAR GASKET

NEOPRENE FOAM RUBBER TAPE

RIBBED FOAM-RUBBER TAPE

METAL SPRING STRIP

VINYL V-STRIP

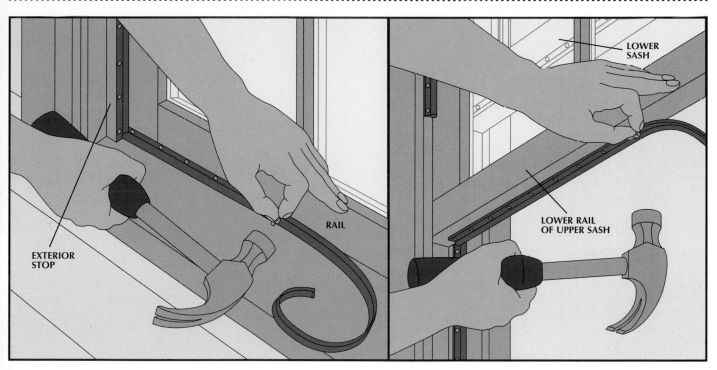

Nailing on tubular gaskets.

◆ Close the sashes. From outside the house, measure and cut lengths of tubular gaskets to fit the top, bottom, and sides of the upper sash; and the bottom and sides of the lower sash.

◆ Nail gaskets to the exterior stops, stretching the strip slightly so the tube-shaped part of the strip is tight and straight against the sash.

◆ Nail a strip along the bottom edge of the lower sash rail *(above, left)* and the top edge of the upper sash rail so the gaskets press tightly against the frame when the window is shut.

◆ Raise the lower sash out of the way and pull down the upper sash, then secure a strip to the underside of the upper sash's bottom rail flush with the inside edge *(above, right)*. This strip will seal the gap between the upper and lower sashes when the window is shut.

Applying adhesive-backed strips.

Adhesive-backed foam stripping works best on friction-free surfaces such as the underside of the bottom rail of lower sashes.

◆ Wipe the window frame clean.

◆ Slowly pull the protective backing off the strip as you press the adhesive against the surface *(left)*.

ATTACHING SPRING STRIPS

1. Measuring the strips.

On double-hung windows, spring strips are installed in the side channels of the upper and lower sashes, on the top and bottom rails of the upper sash, and on the bottom rail of the lower sash. The metal type is shown on this page; vinyl V-strips are installed similarly, but with self-adhesive backing.

◆ For the four side-channel strips, close the upper sash, raise the lower sash, and measure from the bottom of the channel to a point 2 inches above the bottom rail of the upper sash *(right)*. Cut the strips to length with tin snips.

◆ For the sash strips, measure the bottom rail of the lower sash from channel to channel and cut three strips to length.

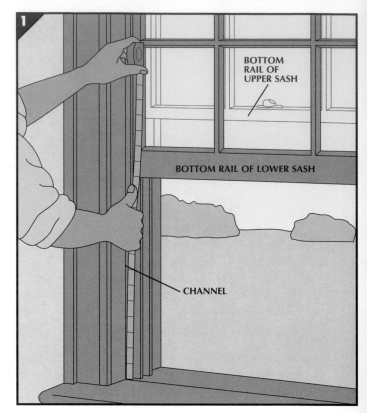

2. Fitting the side-channel strips

◆ Open the lower sash as high as it will go and clean loose paint or dirt from the channels.

◆ With its nailing flange against the inside edge of the channel, slip the end of a lower-sash strip into the gap between the sash and channel *(left)* and slide it up until its bottom end is flush with the bottom of the channel.

◆ Repeat for the opposite lower-sash channel.

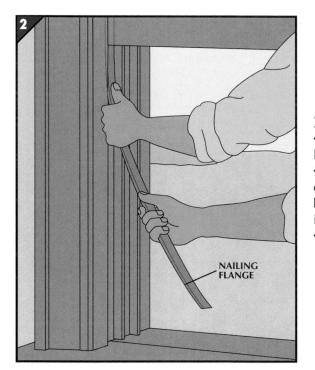

3. Securing the side-channel strips.

◆ Nail each strip to the channel up to the bottom rail of the lower sash *(right)*.

◆ Drop the lower sash and fasten the part of the strips that extend 2 inches above the bottom rail of the upper sash.

◆ Lower the upper sash and install the upper-sash strips in the channels by slipping them into position from the top.

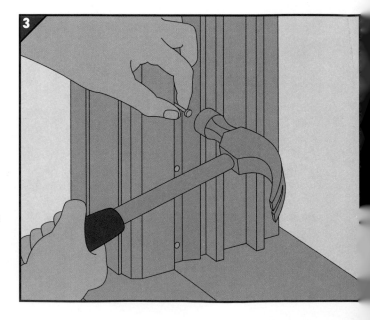

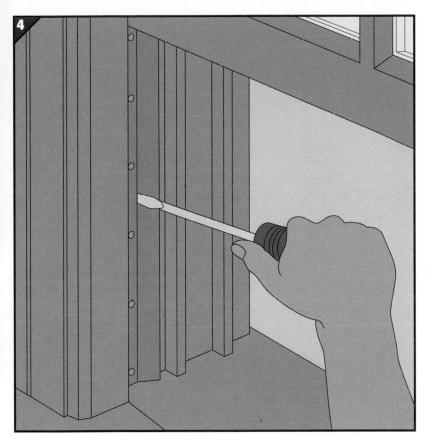

4. Tightening the seal.
With moderate pressure, run a wide-blade screwdriver down the crease in each strip a few times *(left)*, until the strip presses firmly against the sash. This will increase the spring action of the strips, providing a better seal.

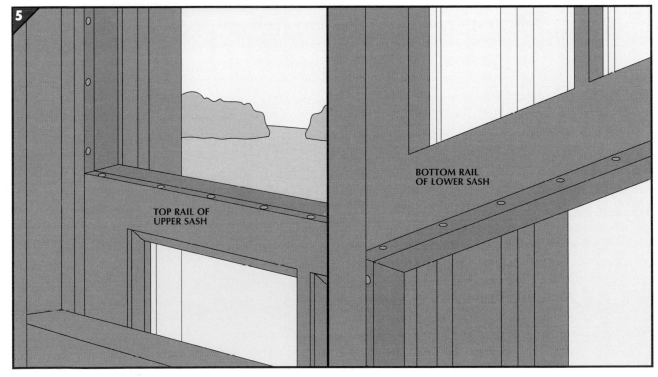

TOP RAIL OF
UPPER SASH

BOTTOM RAIL
OF LOWER SASH

5. Fastening top and bottom strips.
◆ Nail a strip to the top of the upper sash's top rail, positioning the nailing flange along the inside face of the window *(above, left)*. Hammer gently to avoid cracking the glass.
◆ Fasten a strip to the underside of the bottom sash's lower rail *(above, right)*.
◆ Tighten the seal on both strips as shown in Step 4.

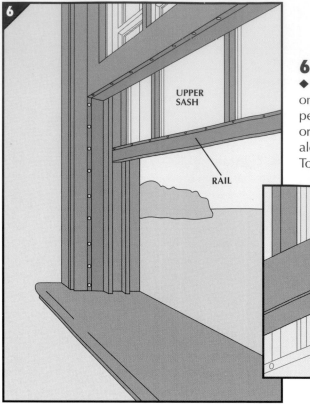

UPPER
SASH

RAIL

6. The center strip.

◆ Secure the last sash strip on the inside face of the upper sash's bottom rail *(left)*; orient the nailing flange along the rail's top edge. To ensure the sashes slide smoothly *(inset)*, sink the nail heads below the surface of the flange by tapping them with a nail set.

◆ Complete the job by tightening the seal of this strip as in Step 4.

COVERING A WINDOW WITH AN INSULATOR KIT

1. Applying the tape.

Insulator kits usually come with a roll of double-sided tape and enough plastic film to cover a large double-hung window.

◆ Clean the window frame of all dust, dirt, and loose paint. Make sure the frame is dry.

◆ Apply a length of tape along each side of the frame.

◆ Trim the ends so there is no gap or overlap.

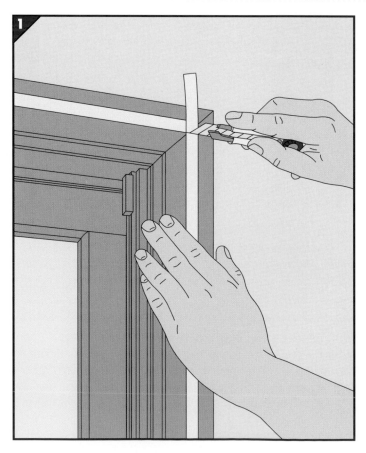

2. Hanging the plastic film.
◆ Measure the distance between the outside edges of the tape strips and add 2 inches to each side. Lay out the plastic film on a flat surface and cut it to size.
◆ Position the film over the opening, pressing it very lightly on the tape. Reposition the film as needed, then press it firmly in place *(left)*.

3. Tightening the film.
Remove all the wrinkles from the film with a blow-dryer set to maximum heat. With the nozzle $\frac{1}{4}$ inch from the film, pass the dryer over the plastic *(right)*. To avoid melting the plastic, keep the dryer in constant motion, and do not let it touch the film.

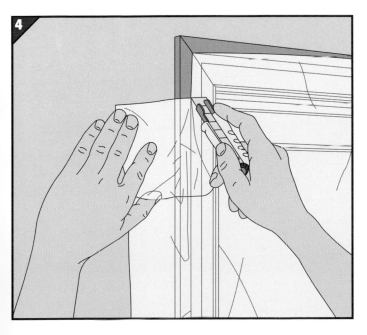

4. Trimming the film.
With a utility knife, cut the film flush with the outside edges of the tape *(left)*.

To remove the film at the end of winter, pull the plastic off the tape, then slowly peel the tape off the window frame.

Sealing metal casements.

Metal casement windows can be weatherproofed with vinyl gaskets that have a deep groove designed to slip easily onto all four sides of the frame.
◆ Trim the gaskets to fit, mitering their ends at 45 degrees.
◆ Apply vinyl-to-metal adhesive to the frame and press the gasket in place *(left)*.

Wood casement windows.

New wood casement windows have built-in weatherproofing, but older ones can be sealed with spring strips *(page 10)*. Fasten the strip with the nailing flange on the outside edge of the frame toward the sash; the window will compress the strip when it closes *(right)*.

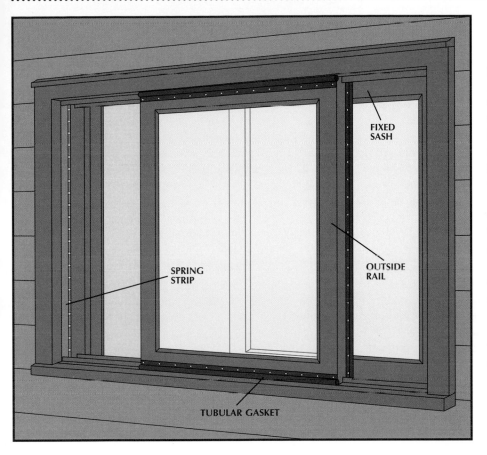

FIXED SASH

SPRING STRIP

OUTSIDE RAIL

TUBULAR GASKET

Sealing sliding windows.

New wood sliding windows have weather stripping built in between the frame and the sash. Older types, however, may need sealing. For windows with one sliding sash *(left)*, seal only the movable part.

◆ Fasten a spring strip in the side channel that the movable sash closes against.

◆ Secure tubular gaskets *(page 9)* to the exterior surface of the sliding sash along the top, bottom, and outside rails. Make sure that the gasket on the outside rail fits snugly against the fixed sash when the window is closed.

If both sashes move, seal the window with spring strips as for a double-hung window *(pages 10-12)*.

REPLACEMENT SASH KITS FOR DOUBLE-HUNG WINDOWS

Fitting replacement sashes from a kit is an easy and effective way to seal timeworn double-hung windows—and at the same time make them operate more smoothly.

In contrast to putting in new windows and frames, very little carpentry is required. First, the sash stops, parting stops, sashes, and any rope-and-pulley system are removed. The jamb-liner clips supplied are then tacked to the jambs, the jamb liners and parting stops are fitted in place, the new sashes are installed, and the old sash stops are nailed to the jambs.

Because these replacement sashes usually have to be custom made to fit the window opening, they can cost almost as much as new windows with frames; however, their ease of installation is a decided advantage.

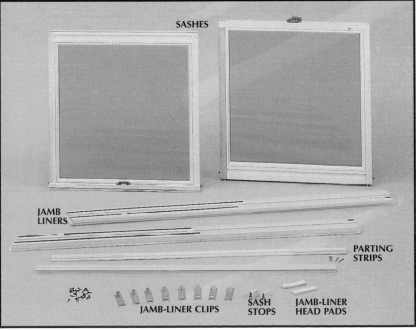

SASHES

JAMB LINERS

PARTING STRIPS

JAMB-LINER CLIPS

SASH STOPS

JAMB-LINER HEAD PADS

Doors cannot be closed as tightly as windows, so they are more difficult to seal. But a variety of products—weather stripping, thresholds, and sweeps—keep air from leaking through.

Straightening a Door: Weather stripping can't do its job properly on a binding door. Before applying any product, adjust the hinges and sand or plane the door edges until the door opens and closes smoothly with a narrow, uniform gap between edges and jamb.

A door may bind because loose hinge screws make it sag. If the screws don't hold, replace them with longer ones. Or, drill out the screw hole, glue in a length of dowel, and bore a new clearance hole for the screw. If this does not solve the problem, plane the binding door edge.

Blocking Door Drafts: Door sweeps and weatherproof thresholds seal the bottom of swinging doors *(pages 18-19)*, while garage doors require a special type of weather stripping to provide a tight seal against uneven concrete floors *(page 19)*.

Simple to apply, self-adhesive V-strips are commonly used to weather-strip doors. These doubled-over strips of vinyl fit between door edges and jambs, filling gaps. V-strips are not as sturdy as door-stop stripping, which can be more tricky to apply. Installation of both products is described opposite.

TOOLS

Hammer
Screwdriver
Pry bar
Utility knife

Tin snips
Hacksaw
Backsaw
Wood chisel
  and mallet

MATERIALS

2 x 4
V-strip weather
  stripping
Door sweep

Door-stop weather
  stripping
Weatherproof
  threshold
Garage door
  weather stripping

SAFETY TIPS

Always wear safety gloggles when driving nails.

WEATHERPROOF
THRESHOLD

U-SHAPED
BOTTOM SWEEP

PLAIN DOOR
SWEEP

WOODEN DOOR-STOP
WEATHER STRIPPING

METAL DOOR-STOP
WEATHER STRIPPING

GARAGE-DOOR
BOTTOM

AN ARRAY OF PRODUCTS

Weatherproof thresholds seal the bottom of doors best, but the easiest product to install is a sweep fastened under or against the bottom edge of a door.

Weather stripping attaches to the jambs at the sides and top—usually to the door-stop molding—so its flexible edges press against the door face when it is closed. You can choose from a variety of shapes depending on the shape and size of gap you need to seal. Widely used products include wood, metal, and plastic door-stop strips edged with plastic tubing or foam, and closed-cell adhesive-backed foam tapes.

Unless the product is self-adhesive, fasteners are generally included in the package. Some products may come with specific installation instructions.

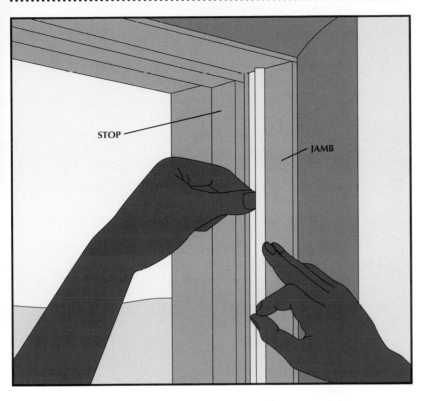

Installing V-stripping.

◆ With a utility knife or tin snips, cut strips for both sides and the top of the door, trimming the pieces as necessary to accommodate the hinges and lock.

◆ Remove the backing paper and position a strip along the jamb with the point of the V facing the door and the other edge about $\frac{1}{8}$ inch from the stop.

◆ Press the strip in place *(left)*.

Attaching door-stop stripping.

◆ With tin snips, cut strips the same length as the stops at the top and sides of the door.

◆ With the door closed, position the top piece against the top stop, lightly pressing the flexible edge against the door.

◆ With a helper holding the stripping in place, slide a piece of paper between the door and the flexible edge—it should barely slide. Adjust the position of the strip as necessary, then nail it to the jamb.

◆ Position the strips along the sides of the door *(right)*, then nail them in place.

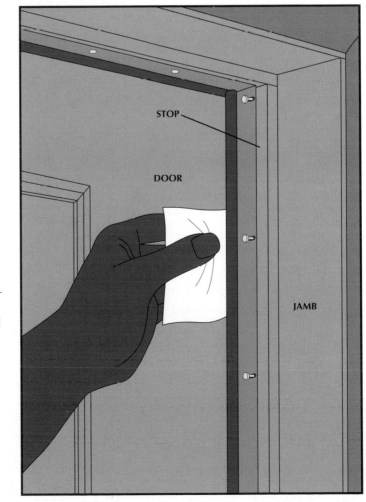

ADDING A DOOR SWEEP

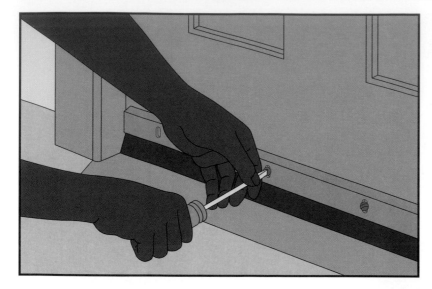

Attaching a standard door sweep.
◆ Working outside with the door closed, measure the width of the door and cut the sweep to length with tin snips.
◆ Position the sweep so it fits snugly against the threshold when the door is shut while allowing the door to operate smoothly.
◆ Screw the sweep to the door *(left)*. The oblong screw holes allow you to adjust the sweep up or down as needed.

Fastening a bottom sweep.
◆ With tin snips, cut the sweep to the width of the door.
◆ Open the door and slip the sweep on the bottom of the door *(right)*. If necessary, adjust the width of the sweep to the door thickness by squeezing the sides together.
◆ Close the door, let the sweep drop onto the threshold, and drive the screws partway into their slots.
◆ Adjust the height of the sweep so it is snug, but not so tight that the door binds. Tighten the screws.

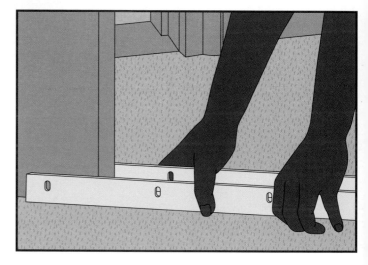

INSTALLING A WEATHERPROOF THRESHOLD

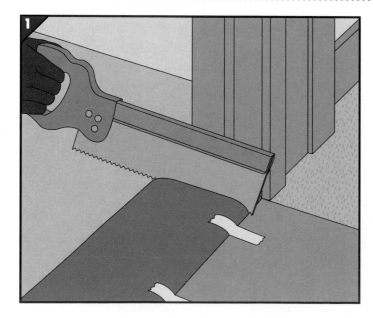

1. Removing the existing threshold.
◆ Cover the floor around the door with pieces of cardboard secured by masking tape.
◆ Try to remove the threshold with a pry bar. If it does not lift up easily, cut through each end with a backsaw *(left)* and pry up the center piece; chip out the rest of the threshold with a chisel and mallet.
◆ Clean the sill.

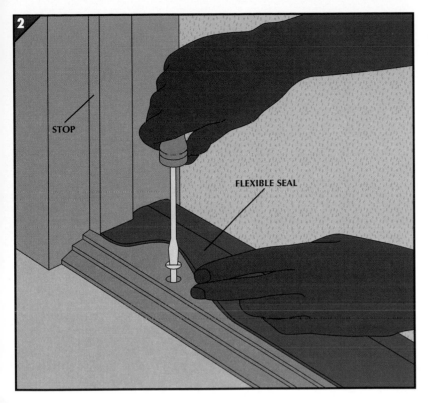

STOP

FLEXIBLE SEAL

2. Fitting the threshold.
◆ With a hacksaw, cut the new threshold to fit snugly between the side jamb. If necessary, trim the door stop with a backsaw or chisel to accommodate the threshold.
◆ Position the threshold so that the flap side of the flexible seal faces away from the door.
◆ Lift up the plastic flap and screw the threshold in place *(left)*.

On some thresholds, the screw holes are exposed. Once the piece is attached, slide the flexible insert into place over the screws.

STRIPS FOR A GARAGE DOOR

Sealing a wood overhead door.
◆ Before installing weather stripping, paint the bottom of the door to protect it against moisture.
◆ Cut the weather stripping to the width of the door with tin snips, a utility knife, or a hacksaw.
◆ Pull the door partway down so the bottom is at a convenient height and brace it on a 2-by-4.
◆ Position the stripping against the door bottom with the flap facing the outside, then nail it in place.

If you have an automatic garage door opener, you may need to recalibrate it to account for the increased door height.

FLAP

Plugging Up the Cracks and Crannies

Because the materials that go into building a house expand and contract at different rates as temperatures change, cracks and gaps are bound to appear at the junction of two different materials. Breaches around windows and doors, and around pipes and wires that pass through walls, can be equivalent to a 2-foot-square vent opening.

Locating Air Leaks: Professionals test a house's air-tightness with a device called a blower door. After shutting all the windows and every door but one, they mount a fan in the open door. As the fan reduces pressure in the house, they locate leaks with smoke sticks. Any draft that stirs smoke is investigated.

You can subject your house to a similar test by opening a door on the leeward side of the house on a windy day. Burn an incense stick to generate the smoke. Or, set up the homemade draft finder shown opposite.

Choosing a Sealant: Dozens of sealant materials are available to close gaps. The characteristics of the most common products are provided in the chart below. Others, such as glazing compound for window panes and special caulk for chimney and ducts, may be required for special applications. Keep in mind that shrinkage is sometimes an advantage, since a caulk that shrinks will become less visible.

Whichever sealant you choose, read the label instructions to ensure it is the best one for the job. Follow the product's safety precautions. Always work in a well-ventilated area when applying toxic materials.

 TOOLS

Caulking gun
Utility knife
Putty knife

Screwdriver
Pry bar
Wood chisel
Sanding block
Paintbrush

 **MATERIALS**

Caulk
Rope caulk
Foam backer rod

Insulating foam
Alcohol
Linseed oil
Window glazing
  compound

 **SAFETY TIPS**

Wear rubber gloves when working with solvent-base glazing compound; wear gloves and goggles when applying insulating foam.

A SEALANT FOR EVERY PURPOSE

Sealant	Special Uses	Durability	Adhesion	Shrinkage
Polybutene Rope Caulk	Temporary sealing	1-2 years	Fair	Moderate
Butyl Rubber Caulk	Metal to masonry	7-10 years	Excellent	Moderate
Polyurethane Caulk	All purposes	20 years	Excellent	Very low
Acrylic Latex Caulk	Indoors and protected areas	2-10 years	Excellent, except to metal	Moderate
Latex Caulk	All purposes	5-15 years	Excellent	Low
Silicone Caulk	All purposes	20 or more years	Excellent	Very low
Silicone/Latex Caulk	All purposes	10-20 years	Excellent	Moderate
Insulating Foam	Large gaps	10 or more years	Excellent	Very low
Foam Backer Rod	Large gaps	10 or more years	None	Very low

Finding gaps and cracks.

The areas of a house where caulk is generally needed are outlined in red in the illustration at left. If your chimney rises along an outside wall, caulk the line at which it meets the siding. One trouble spot not visible in the drawing is the opening through which a pipe or wire enters the living quarters from an unheated attic, basement, or crawl space.

TRICKS OF THE TRADE

A Simple Draft Finder

Locate drafts on a windy day by attaching a sheet of lightweight plastic film to a hanger with clothespins. Close all doors and windows, except one on the leeward side of the house, then pass the film in front of every door and window in turn—any fluttering indicates a draft problem.

urface-Drying Time	Curing Time	Cleaner	Primer	Paint
emains moist and pliant	N/A	None needed	None needed	Should not be painted
4 hours	7 days	Naphtha; paint thinner	None needed	Can be painted
4 hours	7 days	Toluene	Neoprene primer required	Can be painted
$\frac{1}{2}$ hour	3 days	Water	Needed on porous surfaces	Can be painted
$\frac{1}{2}$ hour	5 days	Naphtha; paint thinner	Rarely needed	Can be painted
hour	2-5 days	Naphtha; paint thinner	Check label instructions	Check label instructions
hour	1-5 days	Water	Rarely needed	Can be painted
hour	4 hours	Acetone	None needed	Required outdoors; not needed indoors
/A	N/A	N/A	None	Cover with all-purpose caulk; paint, if desired

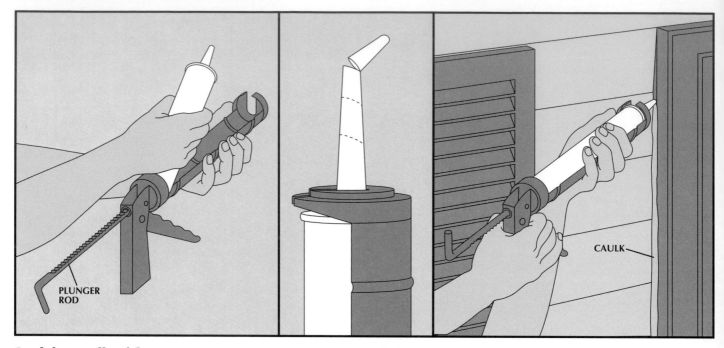

Applying caulk with a gun.

◆ Load a caulking gun by first rotating the plunger rod so its teeth face up, then fully retracting it. Insert the caulk cartridge *(above, left)*, rotate the plunger rod so the teeth face down, and pull on the trigger.

◆ With a utility knife, nip off the tapered nozzle tip at a 45-degree angle, cutting an opening for a thin, medium, or heavy bead *(above, center)*. Push a nail through the tip to puncture the seal at the base of the nozzle.

◆ With the gun at a 45-degree angle to the surface, slide it upward and squeeze the trigger with steady pressure *(above, right)*, producing a smooth, even bead. Where several passes are necessary, release the trigger at the end of each pass and continue to move the gun as you slowly squeeze the trigger to begin the next pass.

◆ To stop the flow of caulk, rotate the plunger rod so its teeth point upward, then pull the rod back 1 or 2 inches.

Fine-Tuning a Caulking Gun

Applying a neat line of caulk in exactly the right place isn't easy. Because caulk cartridges expand under pressure, the caulk may be slow to respond when you squeeze the trigger or may continue to run when you release it. You can overcome such problems by wrapping cartridges with duct tape before loading them—the result is a more accurate caulking job.

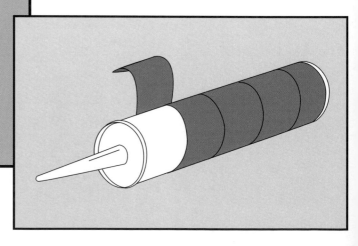

Using a roll-up tube.
◆ Snip the tip off the nozzle as for a cartridge *(opposite)*.
◆ Starting at the bottom of the fixture, apply the sealant by squeezing the tube and moving it upward around the fixture *(right)*.

Applying rope caulk.
Polybutene rope is especially useful for temporary seals and areas that are hard to reach.
◆ Unroll a single or multiple strand, depending on the width of the gap to be sealed.
◆ Press the caulk into the gap with your fingers *(left)*. If the material is sticky, work with wet hands.

Sealing deep cracks.
◆ For a crack more than $\frac{1}{2}$ inch deep—such as at the joint between siding and foundation—push foam backer rod into the gap with a screwdriver or putty knife *(right)*.
◆ Apply one or more beads of sealant over the backer rod with a caulking gun.

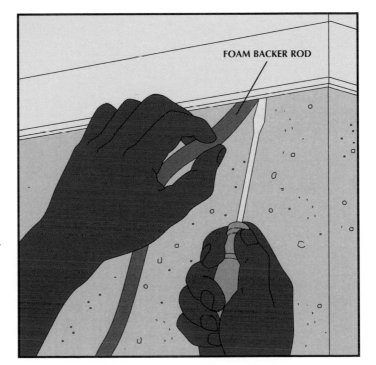

FOAM BACKER ROD

1. Applying insulating foam.

◆ Remove trim around a window or door and clean the surfaces using a cloth dampened with alcohol.

◆ Open windows in the room to provide ventilation and prepare the product according to manufacturer's directions.

◆ Insert the tip of the nozzle into the gap and lightly press the trigger. Fill the space as recommended by the manufacturer—usually less than one-half full. The foam will expand quickly to fill the gap *(above)*.

◆ Release the nozzle about 5 inches from the end of the gap but continue to move the applicator to the end.

2. Trimming the foam.

◆ Let the foam cure for the length of time indicated on the label.

◆ Trim off the excess foam with a sharp putty knife or utility knife *(right)*.

◆ Sand the foam lightly.

REGLAZING WINDOWS

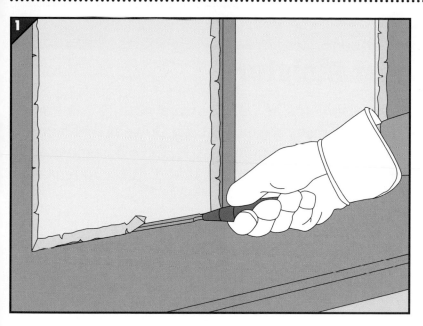

1. Removing the old compound.

◆ Brush the old glazing compound with linseed oil. Let it soak for 30 minutes, then scrape off the softened compound with a stiff-bladed putty knife or chisel *(left)*. If the oil does not soften the compound sufficiently, warm it with a heat gun on a low setting, being careful not to heat the glass.
◆ Sand the channel smooth, then brush it with linseed oil.

> ### ⚠ CAUTION
>
> ### Lead in Glazing Compound
>
> *Old glazing compound may contain lead. When removing it, keep children, pets, and pregnant women away from the area. Cover the ground under the window with newspaper; and wear gloves and a high-efficiency particulate air (HEPA) filter. Spray the compound with water before scraping it off or sanding it, and do any sanding by hand, rather than with a power sander. Dispose of the debris safely.*

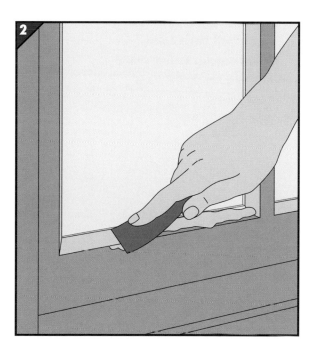

2. Applying new glazing compound.

◆ Roll glazing compound into $\frac{1}{4}$-inch strips and press them against the joints between the glass and frame.
◆ Holding a putty knife at an angle, smooth the compound to a bevel *(left)*. If the knife sticks, dip it in water for a water-base compound or paint thinner for a solvent-base compound.
◆ Let the compound cure as specified on the label, then paint it to match the frame. For a weatherproof seal, extend the line of paint $\frac{1}{16}$ inch onto the surface of the glass.

FOAM OUTLET BACKINGS

Outlets and switches on exterior walls can let a lot of cold air into a house. Precut to suit the most common electrical cover plates, foam pads like these are a simple way to cut down on heat loss. To install a pad, remove the outlet cover plate, position the pad, then refasten the plate.

The Battle Against Moisture

Water seepage can cause serious problems in a home, from peeling paint and a damp basement to rotted framing. In many cases, you can prevent this damage simply by channeling water away from the foundation. Cracks in basement walls can be plugged, and water expelled with a sump pump. In the attic, condensation can be halted by improving ventilation.

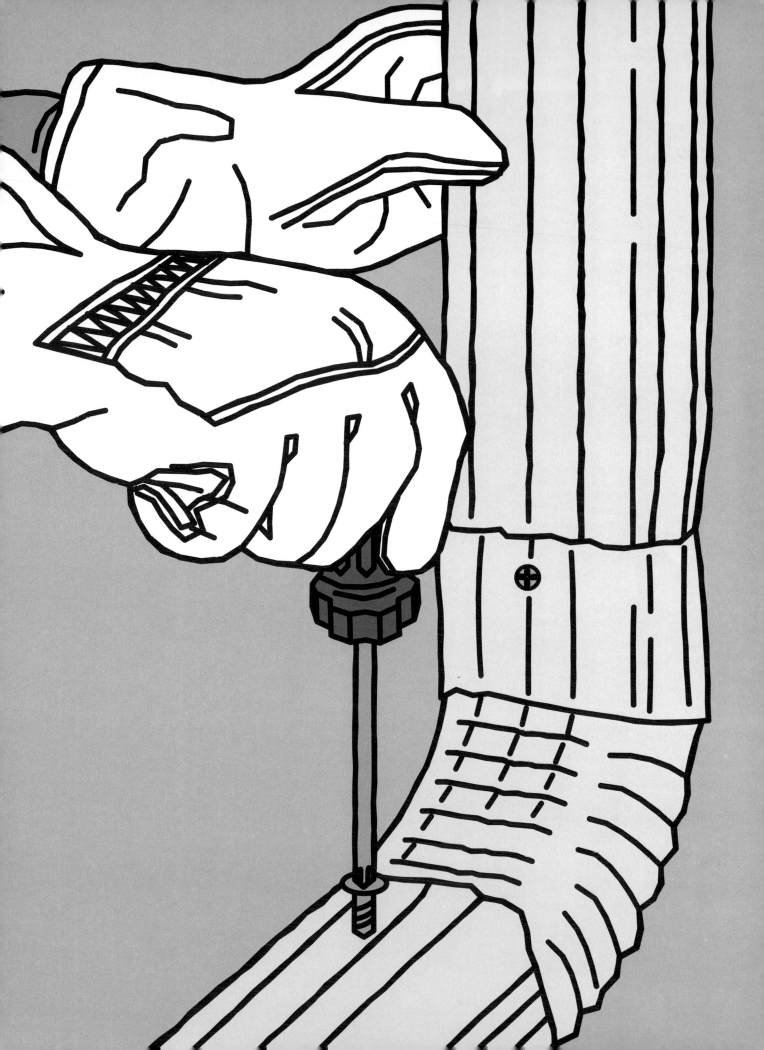

Channeling Water with Gutters and Downspouts

The first place to investigate the cause of a damp basement is not the foundation but the roof—specifically the gutters and downspouts. Properly mounted and well maintained, these channels can often beat a water leakage problem at its source.

Maintaining Gutters: Inspect gutters for blockage *(opposite)* and misalignment *(page 30)* once a year. Immediate inspection is called for if water does not flow well from downspout exits. Leaves from nearby trees can block gutters; leaf guards and strainers are a help *(opposite)*, but need to be cleaned two or three times a year.

Although newer gutters are typically made of aluminum or vinyl, some older ones are steel, and should be checked for corrosion. Small rust patches can be scraped clean with a wire brush, then coated with antirust paint.

Adding New Gutters: If your existing gutters are beyond repair or your home has no gutters, a new system is in order. First determine whether you need a drip edge *(page 35)*. Then refer to the following pages for instructions on installing aluminum gutters.

Estimating Materials: Measure the total length of the eaves, including those above porches and other secondary roofs. Add a slip-joint connector for every 10 feet (the standard length of gutter sections), end caps for the ends of each run, and inside and outside corner pieces as necessary. You'll also need drop outlets to accommodate the downspouts. One downspout can drain up to 40 feet of gutter; for longer runs, position a downspout at each end and slope the gutter sections from the middle. To calculate downspout lengths, measure the height of your walls from the ground to the eaves; include three elbow connectors for each downspout and a downspout band every 10 feet. Your supplier will help you determine how much to budget for waste and provide the best sealant to join the parts.

Working Safely at Heights: Installation is done mostly from a ladder. Follow the precautions presented in the box below for working safely aboveground.

TOOLS

Tape measure
Chalk line
Line level
Hammer
Screwdriver
Pliers
Putty knife
Utility knife
Tin snips
Hacksaw
File
Trap-and-drain auger
Caulking gun
Electric drill

MATERIALS

Common nails ($2\frac{1}{2}$")
Galvanized wood
  screws ($1\frac{1}{2}$" No. 6)
Galvanized sheet-
  metal screws
  ($\frac{3}{8}$" No. 8)
Spikes and ferrules
Roofing nails ($1\frac{1}{4}$")
Wire
Aluminum gutter
  system
Gutter sealant
Drip edge
Antirust paint
Leaf strainer
Leaf guard

SAFETY TIPS

Wear goggles when driving nails. Put on work gloves when handling aluminum gutters and rubber gloves when cleaning out gutters.

LADDER SAFETY

✔ Keep ladders away from overhead electric wires.

✔ Push the spreaders of a stepladder all the way down to the locked position. Never use a stepladder folded up.

✔ Always lean an extension ladder against the wall so the distance between the foot of the ladder and the wall is one-quarter the distance the ladder extends up the wall. Never prop it against a window or door.

✔ Make sure the ladder is level; place the feet on a board if necessary.

✔ As you climb an extension ladder, have someone steady it, and hold the rungs with both hands. Don't carry anything in your hands while climbing; wear a tool belt containing your tools and supplies instead.

✔ Don't stand above the second-highest rung of a stepladder or the third-highest step of an extension one.

✔ Don't overreach to either side of the ladder and never step from one ladder to another.

GUTTER MAINTENANCE

Unclogging a downspout.
First try removing debris from a clogged downspout by hand or by flushing it with a garden hose. If these methods don't work, use a plumber's trap-and-drain auger.
◆ Feed the end of the auger's coil into the downspout as far as possible, then lock the handle.
◆ Slowly turn the handle clockwise *(right)*. When the handle moves easily, feed in more coil and repeat.
◆ Once the downspout is clear of debris, flush it with water.

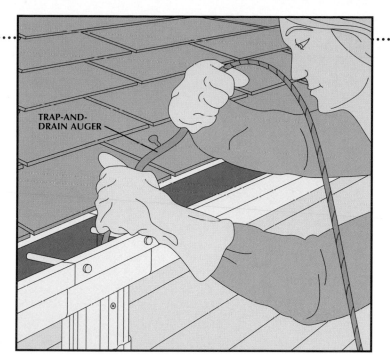

TRAP-AND-DRAIN AUGER

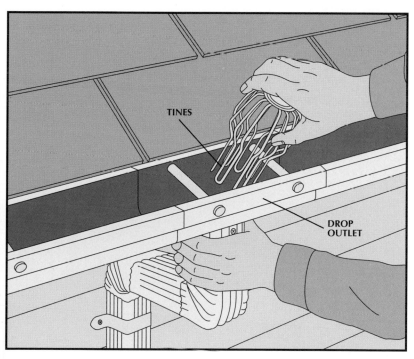

TINES

DROP OUTLET

Adding a leaf strainer.
◆ Adjust the strainer to fit the drop outlet snugly by squeezing or expanding the tines.
◆ Fit it into the drop outlet *(left)*.

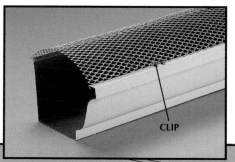

CLIP

Fitting a leaf guard.
◆ Cut the guard to length; use a utility knife on plastic, tin snips on metal.
◆ Fold the material across its width into a cylindrical shape and fit it between the edge of the roof and the inside lip of the gutter *(right)*.

Some types of leaf guard are secured to the outside of the gutter with clips *(photograph)*.

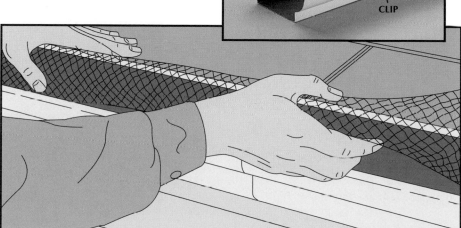

STRAIGHTENING A CROOKED GUTTER

1. Checking for misalignment.

To determine whether a gutter is bent out of alignment, hose water onto the roof, directing the spray from side to side *(above)*. Watch the flow of water in the gutter; if the gutter is misaligned, water will pool in the low spots.

2. Realigning the gutter.

◆ On a gutter fastened by spikes and ferrules *(page 33)*, twist the spikes free with locking-grip pliers *(right)*; remove the ferrules.
◆ Reposition the gutter to raise the low spots and fasten the spikes and ferrules *(page 32, Step 5)*. If more support is necessary, drive additional spikes and ferrules into adjacent rafter ends.

For a fascia bracket or wraparound hanger *(page 33)*, remove the hanger to align the gutter, then reposition the hanger. Replace a badly bent hanger.

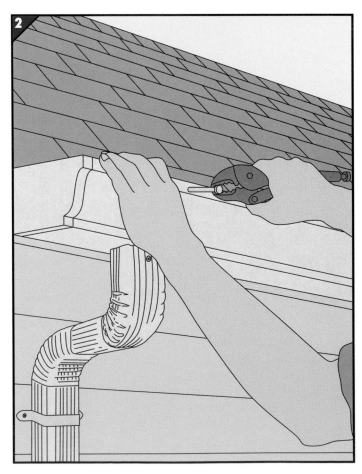

1. Marking the gutter's slope.
◆ At the end of the house where you will locate the high end of the gutter, tack a nail into the fascia, $\frac{3}{4}$ inch below its top edge.
◆ Stretch a chalk line to the opposite end of the fascia and level it with a line level; mark this point on the fascia. Make a second mark below the first to indicate the required slope: $\frac{1}{4}$ inch for every 20 feet of run. Tack another nail into the fascia at the second mark and secure the chalk line to the two nails, keeping the line taut.
◆ Position yourself at the middle of the chalk line and snap it to mark the top edge of the gutter (left).

2. Adding end caps.
◆ With a caulking gun, apply a band of gutter sealant along the inside edges of the end cap.
◆ Push the cap onto the gutter (right). Smooth any squeezed-out sealant with a putty knife.

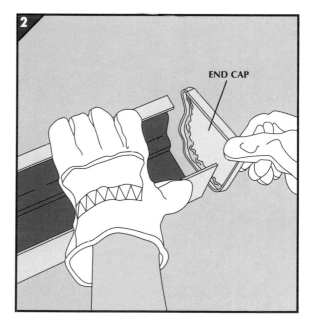

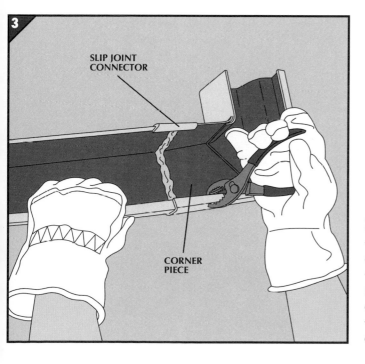

3. Fitting corner pieces and drop outlets.
◆ Apply a wide band of sealant along the middle of a slip-joint connector.
◆ Center the connector over the ends of the corner piece or drop outlet and the gutter. Butt the ends together and press them into the sealant.
◆ Crimp the ends of the connector around the edges of the joined pieces with pliers (left).

4. Hanging the gutter.

◆ Mark the points where the rafters meet the fascia—usually where the nails secure the fascia to the rafters.

◆ To avoid joining sections of gutter from a ladder, join them on the ground with connectors, using the technique shown in Step 3.

◆ Loop wire around the ends of the gutter.

◆ Just above the chalk line, drive a $2\frac{1}{2}$-inch nail through the fascia into a rafter end at each end of the run.

◆ With a helper, lift the gutter into position and hang the wire loops from the nails *(above)*.

5. Securing the gutter.

◆ Fit a ferrule inside the gutter in line with a rafter end.

◆ Tap a spike through the gutter into the ferrule *(right)*.

◆ With the top edge of the gutter even with the chalk line, drive the spike so its head is flush with the outside of the gutter.

◆ Secure the gutter at every second rafter. In areas with heavy snowfall, fasten it to every rafter.

FERRULE

SPIKE

THREE WAYS TO HANG GUTTERS

Strong and easy to install, the spike and ferrule *(left)* is the most common gutter fastener. The ferrule is fitted into the gutter and the spike is driven through the ferrule and fascia board into a rafter end.

Fascia brackets *(center)* are less conspicuous than other fasteners. They are nailed to the fascia and the gutter sections are then snapped over them.

While a bit weaker than the other systems, wraparound hangers *(right)* can secure gutters to houses lacking fascia boards. They are fastened to the roof with a nailing strap placed under the roofing material at the eaves.

INSTALLING A DOWNSPOUT

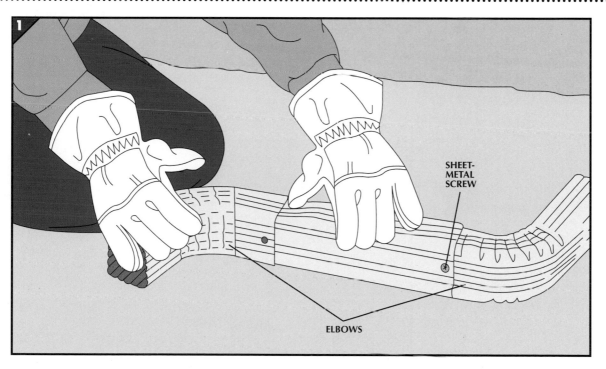

SHEET-METAL SCREW

ELBOWS

1. Preparing the top section.

◆ With a hacksaw, cut a section of downspout long enough to reach from the drop outlet to the wall. File off burrs.

◆ Fit elbows to both ends of this section, sliding the wide end of each piece into the narrow end of its mate *(above)*.

◆ Secure the assembly by first drilling a $\frac{1}{8}$-inch pilot hole through each joint, then driving $\frac{3}{8}$-inch No. 8 galvanized sheet-metal screws into the holes.

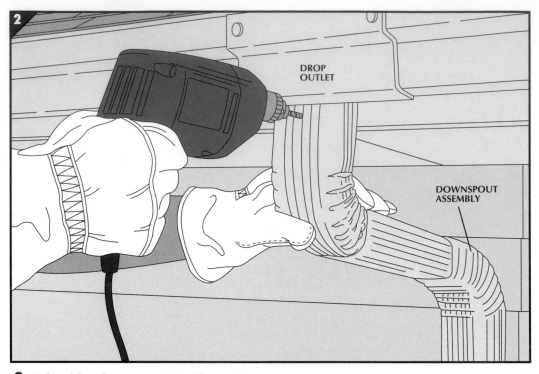

2. Tying the downspout to the gutter.
◆ Slide the top of the downspout assembly onto the drop outlet.
◆ Drill a $\frac{1}{8}$-inch pilot hole through the assembly and the drop outlet *(above)*, and screw the pieces together.
◆ Fasten straight lengths of downspout to the assembly with screws. If you will be adding an extension *(opposite)*, end the downspout 18 inches above the ground. For a splashblock *(opposite)*, locate the bottom of the downspout just above the block. If you plan to connect the downspout to an underground drainage system *(pages 36-37)*, end it about 6 inches above the ground.

3. Anchoring the downspout.
◆ Bend a downspout band around the downspout at both the top and bottom and every 10 feet in between.
◆ Fasten the bands to the wall with $1\frac{1}{2}$-inch No. 6 galvanized wood screws *(right)*.

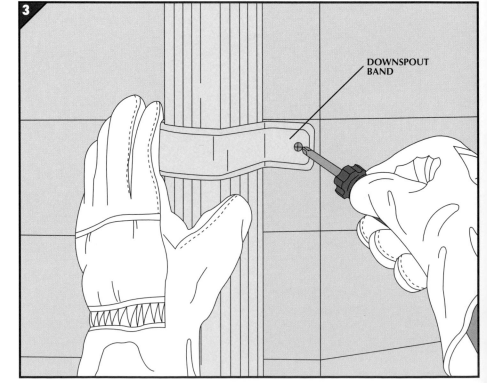

4. Attaching an extension.

◆ Attach an elbow section to the bottom of the downspout with screws.

◆ Add a 3- to 6-foot extension to the elbow *(right)*—the greater the slope of the ground away from the house, the shorter the extension.

An alternative to an extension is a splashblock *(photograph)*. Attach an elbow to the bottom of the downspout and position the block underneath it.

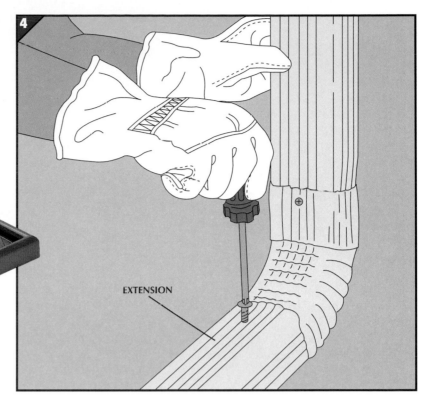

EXTENSION

PROTECTING THE EAVES

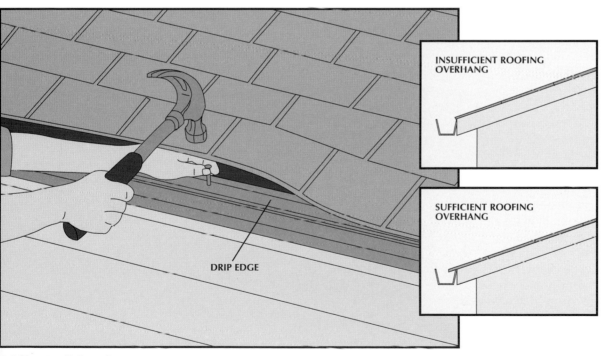

INSUFFICIENT ROOFING OVERHANG

SUFFICIENT ROOFING OVERHANG

DRIP EDGE

Adding a drip edge.

If the roofing material does not overhang the gutter by at least 1 inch *(insets)*, a drip edge is needed on the eaves to direct water runoff into the gutters. The following instructions apply to asphalt shingles; for other types of roofing consult a professional roofer.

◆ Lift the doubled course of shingles at the eave; slide a putty knife underneath to free them if necessary.

◆ Slide the drip edge between the shingles and the roofing felt so its front edge rests against the fascia.

◆ Fasten the drip edge every 12 inches with $1\frac{1}{4}$-inch roofing nails.

Even the most carefully maintained gutters may be ineffective against basement flooding if the earth near the foundation is porous. Gutter extensions and splash blocks cannot accomplish their purpose when the water seeps toward the basement. A long extension of 6 or more feet can help, but may get in the way of lawn mowers and foot traffic.

A Hidden Solution: A more effective method of conveying water away from the foundation is through perforated pipe—generally referred to as drain tile—

attached to the downspout and buried underground. You will need a flexible plastic adapter to join the downspout to the tile. The pipe allows water to percolate into the ground along its length. If your lot slopes, the pipe can end at ground level or at a culvert.

⚠ **CAUTION** *Before excavating, establish the locations of underground obstacles such as electric, water, and sewer lines, and dry wells, septic tanks, and cesspools.*

 TOOLS

Tape measure
Maul
Screwdriver

Garden spade
Pointed shovel
Hacksaw
Electric drill

 **MATERIALS**

Wooden stakes
Galvanized sheet-
  metal screws
  ($\frac{3}{8}$" No. 8)

Gravel
Downspout-to-tile
  adapter
Perforated plastic
  drain tile

1. Digging the ditch.
◆ Remove any extensions or end pieces from the bottom of the downspout. If necessary, add a straight piece of downspout to extend it to about 6 inches above the ground.
◆ Mark the ditch by driving two stakes into the ground, one alongside the house near the downspout and the second in a straight line 12 feet away.
◆ With a garden spade, remove the sod in a 12-inch-wide swath between the stakes, centered on the downspout.
◆ Switch to a pointed shovel and dig a ditch 12 inches deep at the house and sloping to 24 inches deep at the end. Keep the sod and soil for backfilling *(Step 3).*
◆ Line the ditch with 2 to 4 inches of clean drainage gravel.

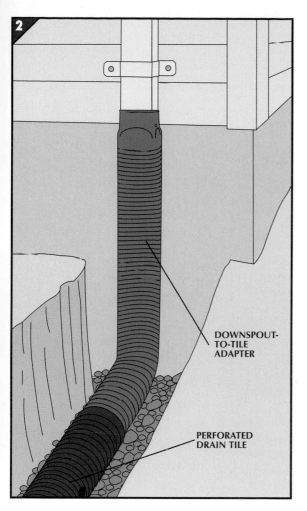

2. Installing the drain tile.

◆ Stretch out a tile-to-downspout adapter to the desired length and push it onto the end of the downspout.

◆ Drill a hole on each side at the end of the downspout and secure the adapter with $\frac{3}{8}$-inch No. 8 galvanized sheet-metal screws.

◆ Fit the end of a length of 3- to 4-inch perforated drain tile around the adapter, then lay the tile in the ditch (left).

DOWNSPOUT-TO-TILE ADAPTER

PERFORATED DRAIN TILE

3. Backfilling the ditch.

◆ Cover the drain tile with 4 inches of gravel (right).

◆ Starting at the end nearest the house, backfill the ditch with the soil you removed.

◆ Lay the sod back in place and tamp the pieces down with your foot.

Diverting Water from Foundations

In general, the ground around a house should slope away from the foundation 1 to 2 inches per foot for a distance of about 4 feet. If the ground slopes toward the foundation, water may seep into the basement.

Regrading: One solution involves building up—or regrading—the area around the house *(below and opposite)*. Since regrading can mean shifting a large amount of earth—1 ton per linear foot of wall—check the ground near the house for areas where water pools after a rain, and try to remedy the problem by dealing with the worst areas first. Use only clean fill dirt—topsoil contains too much organic matter—and do not pile it closer than 8 inches to wood siding.

A Shallow Drainage System: If the lot rises sharply near the house, regrading may be impossible. In this case, you may be able to divert water from the foundation with a shallow drainage system *(pages 39-40)*.

Adding Window Wells: Where dirt is close to a basement window, a window well can prevent water from seeping in *(page 41)*.

A System of Ditches: For a lot that slopes steeply toward the house, a system of swales—ditches that are planted over with grass and so shallow they are almost unnoticeable—will reroute runoff away from the foundation *(page 42)*.

⚠ **CAUTION** *Before excavating, establish the locations of underground obstacles such as electric, water, and sewer lines, and dry wells, septic tanks, and cesspools.*

 TOOLS
Tape measure
Line level
Maul
Shovel
Tamper
Paintbrush
Caulking
  gun

 **MATERIALS**
Wooden stakes
Masonry nails (2")
  and washers
String
Gravel
Fill dirt
Sod
Landscaping fabric
Galvanized window
  well liner
Polyethylene
  sheeting
Asphalt sealant
Sealant for metal
  to masonry

 **SAFETY TIPS**
Wear goggles when nailing. Put on work gloves when handling metal window well liners.

REGRADING A FOUNDATION

1. Measuring the slope.

◆ Drive a stake at the wall and another 4 feet out.

◆ Tie a string to the stake at the wall 8 inches above the ground. Stretch the string to the outer stake, level it with a line level, and tie it to the stake.

◆ Measure the height of the string on the outer stake. If it is 12 inches or more, the slope is adequate. If not, lay out the new slope as follows:

◆ At the outer stake, tie a second string at ground level, then position the first string 8 inches above the ground. Level the first string again and tie it to the stake at the wall, then tie the second string to the stake at the house at the same point. The second string will provide the new slope.

◆ Lay out the slope the same way every 8 feet along the wall.

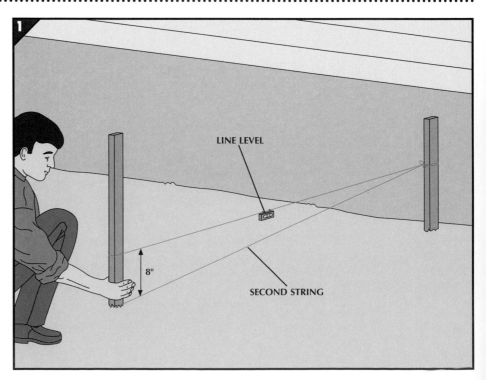

LINE LEVEL

8"

SECOND STRING

2. Building up the slope.

You can spread the fill on the sod or remove the sod and place it on top of the dirt when the job is done. Remove all other organic debris from the area being graded and trim the lowest branches of any shrubs as necessary. If a window will be near the new ground level, add a window-well liner *(page 41).*

◆ Spreading one wheelbarrow-load at a time, build up the soil to the level of the strings *(left)*. Compact the soil with a tamper as you spread it.

◆ To prevent the newly graded ground from eroding, cover it with sod.

CREATING A SHALLOW WATER DIVERSION

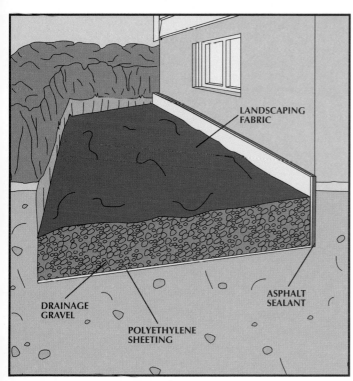

LANDSCAPING FABRIC

DRAINAGE GRAVEL

POLYETHYLENE SHEETING

ASPHALT SEALANT

Anatomy of a water diversion.

This system is designed to draw rainwater and runoff away from the house and allow it to percolate into the soil. The trench is 3 feet wide and 1 foot deep at the wall and slopes away from the foundation. The foundation wall is waterproofed with a coating of asphalt sealant. Polyethylene sheeting is then bonded to the wall and laid along the bottom of the trench. To allow the water to seep down, a 6-inch layer of drainage gravel is placed on top of the sheeting, and landscaping fabric is laid on top of the gravel.

TRICKS OF THE TRADE

Raising a Well Liner

When building up the soil, slope the new fill away from any existing window-well liners as you would from the foundation wall. If the liner is not tall enough, you can extend it by placing bricks on end around its perimeter. Butt the bricks against the well as shown with at least one-third of their length below the level of the new fill. Pack the dirt in place.

1. Excavating the trench.

◆ Begin by removing any sod or vegetation from the area to be excavated.

◆ Dig the trench 3 feet wide and 1 foot deep at the wall, with a level bottom. Tamp the floor of the trench, then smooth it with the back of the shovel.

◆ Mark the slope by driving a stake into the ground at the wall and another at the edge of the trench, then tying a string between the stakes 3 inches above the ground at the wall and at the bottom of the outer stake. Repeat at 8-foot intervals along the trench.

◆ Backfill the trench to the level of the strings with the excavated soil *(left)*.

2. Compacting the soil.

◆ Compact the soil with a tamper *(right)*, shaping it to follow the slope as indicated by the strings. Add soil as necessary.

◆ Brush a coating of asphalt sealant onto the foundation wall from the bottom of the trench to a height 4 inches above the top of the trench.

POLYETHYLENE

GRAVEL

3. Finishing the trench.

◆ While the asphalt is still tacky, press a sheet of polyethylene against the wall and down along the bottom of the trench.

◆ Cover the polyethylene with a 6-inch layer of clean drainage gravel *(left)*.

◆ Cover the gravel with landscaping fabric and backfill the trench.

INSTALLING A WINDOW-WELL LINER

MARK FOR
TOP OF
FLANGE

FLANGE

1. Positioning the well liner.

◆ Buy a galvanized window-well liner slightly wider than the window.
◆ Mark the foundation wall 4 inches above ground level on each side of the window, then dig a hole 3 to 4 feet deep, sized to accommodate the liner.

◆ Set the liner in the hole against the wall (above). Align the top of the flanges with the marks on the wall, then mark the bottom of the liner on the wall. Remove the liner.
◆ Place gravel in the hole up to the lower set of marks.

2. Securing the liner.

◆ Fasten the liner to the wall with 2-inch masonry nails and washers (inset).
◆ Seal the joint between the flange and the wall with a sealant rated for belowground use.
◆ Backfill around the outside of the liner with soil excavated in Step 1 (above). Slope the soil away from the liner.
◆ Fill the liner with gravel to 6 inches from the bottom of the window.
◆ For extra protection, you can fit a ready-made clear plastic cover over the liner.

A SYSTEM OF SWALES AND BERMS

SWALES

1. Laying out a design.
Plan swales to cut across slopes above your house and intercept water flowing downhill. Make the swales long enough to divert the water around and away from the foundation.

Two designs are illustrated above. The house at the bottom of the hill requires only a single curved swale. The house farther up the hill, however, needs a more elaborate system to direct water away from its downhill neighbor.

2. Creating a swale.
◆ Dig a ditch about 2 feet wide and 6 to 10 inches deep, piling and smoothing the dirt on the downhill side of the ditch to form a berm—a lip that will help trap water in the ditch.
◆ Spread 2 to 3 inches of gravel in the ditch, then fill it partway with topsoil.
◆ Place sod over the soil to hold the topsoil and gravel in place.

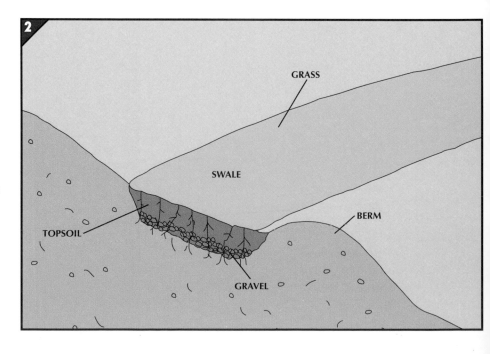

GRASS

SWALE

BERM

TOPSOIL

GRAVEL

Plugging Leaks In a Damp Basement

Water can enter basements by several paths. On a rainy day, it may seep through the walls or stream in through cracks and holes in the foundation. But dampness is not always caused by water coming in from outside; basements are generally cooler than the rooms upstairs, so moisture may condense on the walls. Some simple fixes are shown on the following pages, but if your problem is one of the few caused by an underground source that cannot be corrected, you may need to install a sump pump *(pages 50-53)*.

Solutions for Damp Walls: Conduct the test below to determine the source of the dampness. If condensation is the cause, try a dehumidifier. Minor seepage through walls can often be cured by attention to gutters and downspouts *(pages 28-37)*, or by diverting water away from the foundation *(pages 38-43)*. When gutters and grading are in good shape and walls are still slightly damp, the solution may be to coat them with waterproof cement paint.

Sealing Wall Cracks: The location, orientation, and movement of a crack are all clues to its severity *(page 44)*, and will help you determine whether to fix the crack *(pages 45-48)* or consult a structural engineer. Even dry cracks should be investigated—they could indicate a weakened foundation. If you will have to dig deeper than 2 feet to repair an underground crack *(page 48)*, you may want to have a professional repair it.

TOOLS

Tape measure
Paintbrush
Heat gun
Stiff fiber brush
Putty knife
Cold chisel

Ball-peen hammer
Mason's hawk
Pointing trowel
Caulking gun
Garden spade
Posthole digger
Shovel
Compass saw

MATERIALS

Polyethylene sheeting
Duct tape
Latex concrete-patching
   compound
Bonding agent
Foam backer rod

Flexible masonry
   sealant
Rubber hose
Hydraulic cement
Cylindrical
   cardboard form
Granular bentonite
2 x 4

SAFETY TIPS

Wear gloves and a long-sleeved shirt when working with concrete patching materials. Protect your eyes with goggles when chipping out loose concrete.

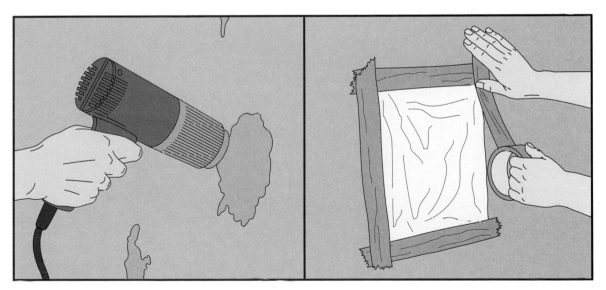

Testing for the source of dampness.
◆ Dry a 12-inch-square section of the damp wall with a heat gun or blow-dryer *(above, left)*.
◆ Cut a slightly smaller square piece of polyethylene sheeting or aluminum foil and fasten it to the wall with duct tape *(above, right)*, sealing all edges to keep out air.

◆ Leave the piece of sheeting or foil in place for 24 hours, then check it for moisture. If the exposed side is wet, then condensation is the problem. If the side against the wall is wet, the problem is seepage. If it is damp on both sides, you likely have both problems.

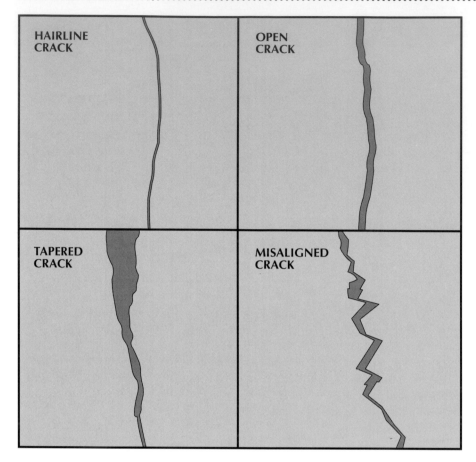

HAIRLINE CRACK

OPEN CRACK

TAPERED CRACK

MISALIGNED CRACK

Evaluating foundation wall cracks.

A crack in a foundation wall can point to a serious structural problem, and should be evaluated carefully. A crack is evidence of movement, usually from settlement or expansion and contraction as a result of temperature fluctuations. Four basic types are shown at left. A hairline crack or an open crack is usually not serious if it is vertical and its edges are aligned and no more than $\frac{1}{8}$ inch apart *(upper left and right)*. However, a crack can be serious if it is horizontal or its edges are tapered, misaligned, or farther apart than $\frac{1}{8}$ inch *(lower left and right)*. Such cracks warrant an inspection by a building professional or structural engineer. If you determine that the crack is not serious, monitor it to find out whether it is stationary or moving *(below)*, then seal the crack using one of the techniques on the following pages.

Monitoring a crack.

◆ If the crack is leaking water, plug it first *(page 48)*.
◆ With a felt-tip pen, mark the crack. Start with a length mark at each end and, across the crack, draw an alignment line a few inches long with width marks at each end *(right)*.
◆ Measure and record the distance between the width and length marks, then monitor the crack for six months.
◆ Consult a building professional if the crack widens by more than $\frac{1}{8}$ inch, lengthens by more than $\frac{1}{4}$ inch, or the alignment line shifts. If the crack is stable, repair it as shown opposite and on page 46; when it has widened or lengthened only slightly, repair it as illustrated on page 47.

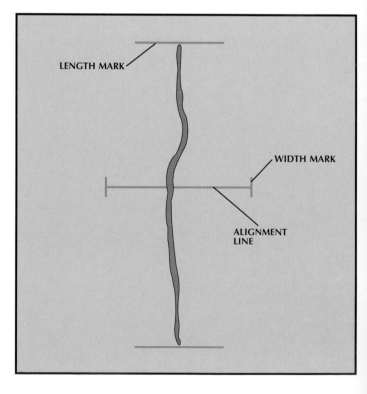

LENGTH MARK

WIDTH MARK

ALIGNMENT LINE

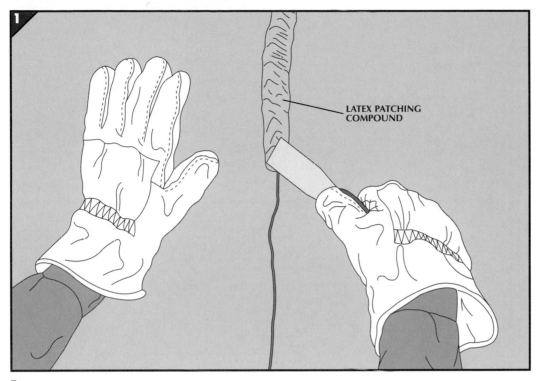

LATEX PATCHING
COMPOUND

1. Applying compound.
◆ Clean the crack with a stiff fiber brush.
◆ Prepare enough latex concrete-patching compound and brush on a bonding agent if recommended by the manufacturer.

◆ Starting at the top of the crack, spread compound into the crack with a putty knife *(above)*.
◆ With the tip of the knife, press the compound into the crack, overfilling it slightly.

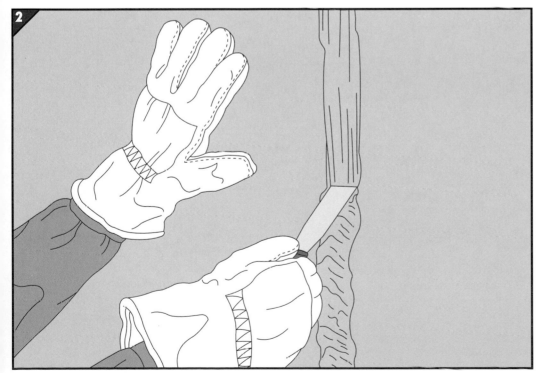

2. Smoothing the patch.
◆ Once the crack is full, draw the putty knife along the compound to smooth it flush against the wall.
◆ Tape polyethylene sheeting over the patch and let it cure for the length of time specified by the manufacturer.

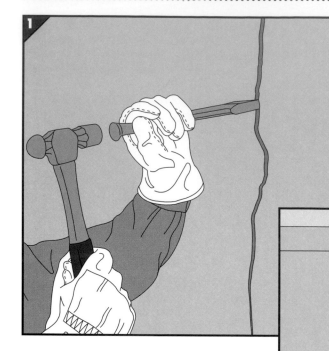

1. Preparing the crack.

◆ Chip any loose concrete from the crack with a cold chisel and a ball-peen hammer *(left)*.

◆ With the chisel and hammer, enlarge the crack to at least $\frac{1}{4}$ inch wide and $\frac{1}{2}$ inch deep. Try to undercut the opening *(inset, left)*; if you can't, cut the sides straight *(inset, right)*. Avoid cutting a V-shaped opening. If you reach a steel reinforcing bar—or rebar—chisel out about 1 inch of concrete behind it.

◆ Clean out the crack with a stiff fiber brush.

2. Applying patching compound.

◆ Prepare a latex concrete-patching compound following the manufacturer's directions. If necessary, dampen the crack with water or brush on a bonding agent.

◆ Place the patching compound on a mason's hawk. Then, holding the hawk against the wall at the bottom of the crack, pack the compound firmly into it with a pointing trowel *(right)*. Gradually move the hawk up the wall, over-filling the crack slightly. Add enough compound to fill the cavity behind any rebar.

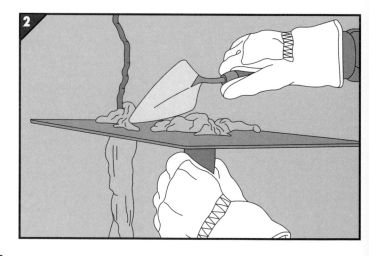

3. Finishing the patch.

◆ Starting at the top of the patch, draw the edge of the trowel along it, scraping off the excess compound onto the mason's hawk *(left)*.

◆ Draw the back of the trowel along the patch to smooth it, working from top to bottom in an arc.

◆ Tape polyethylene sheeting over the patch and let it cure.

SEALING A MOVING BREACH

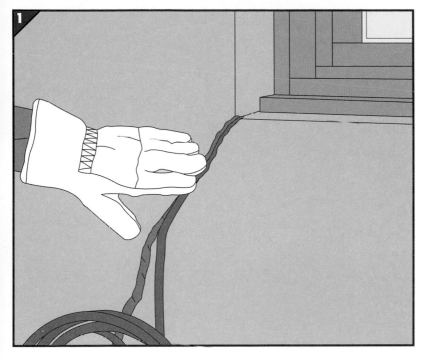

1. Preparing the crack.

A moving crack must be treated with an elastic filler, formulated for masonry, that will move rather than break when the wall shifts.

◆ Chisel away any loose concrete from the crack, then widen it as shown on page 46. Clean out the crack with a stiff fiber brush.

◆ For a crack shallower than $\frac{1}{2}$ inch deep, apply sealant *(Step 2)*; otherwise, fill most of the gap with a length of foam backer rod slightly wider than the crack *(left)*. Push the rod into the crack so it sits $\frac{1}{4}$ inch below the surface; if necessary, use a screwdriver to pack it in. Then fill to the wall surface with sealant *(Step 2)*.

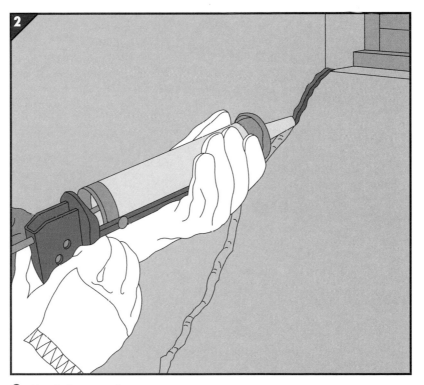

2. Applying sealant.

◆ Load a caulking gun with the sealant.

◆ Starting at the bottom of the crack and holding the gun at a 45-degree angle to the wall, push the tip of the tube into the crack and squeeze the trigger.

Move the gun up the wall to inject a continuous bead of sealant into the crack *(above)*.

◆ Stop once you reach the top; repeat if necessary to fill the crack.

◆ While the sealant is still pliable, smooth it with a wet putty knife.

STOPPING A LEAK

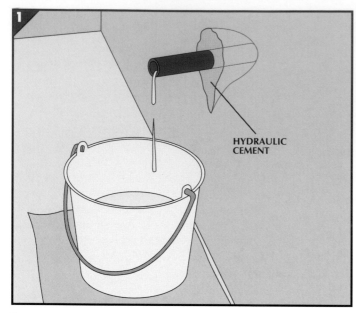

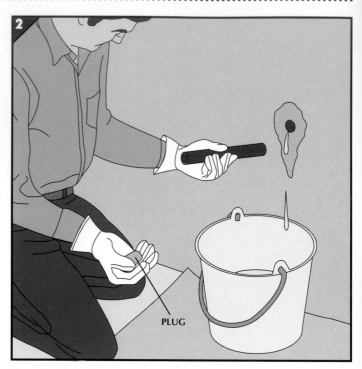

HYDRAULIC CEMENT

PLUG

1. Inserting a bleeder hose.

Cracks and holes that are seeping water can be repaired with hydraulic cement, which hardens in the presence of water.
◆ Insert a short piece of rubber hose—any size that fits—into the leaking crack or hole, and place a bucket under it.
◆ Fill the gaps around the hose with dry hydraulic cement.
◆ Wait a minute or two until the cement sets.

2. Inserting a plug.

◆ To a small amount of hydraulic cement, add water a few drops at a time until the cement is malleable enough to shape into a conical plug.
◆ Pull out the bleeder hose *(above)* and jam the plug into the hole. Hold it in place until the cement sets.
◆ Find and correct the source of the water.

WATERPROOFING AN EXTERIOR CRACK

1. Excavating around the crack.

An underground crack can be effectively blocked with granular bentonite—a clay product that swells on contact with water—available from a construction or industrial chemical supplier.
◆ Once you've patched the aboveground part of a crack *(pages 45 to 47)*, remove any sod or vegetation from the ground around the crack with a garden spade.
◆ With a posthole digger, dig a hole along the crack *(left)* until you uncover its bottom end.
◆ Scrape earth off the wall around the crack and let the wall dry.

⚠ **CAUTION**

Before excavation, establish the locations of underground obstacles such as electric, water, and sewer lines, and lines to dry wells, septic tanks, and cesspools.

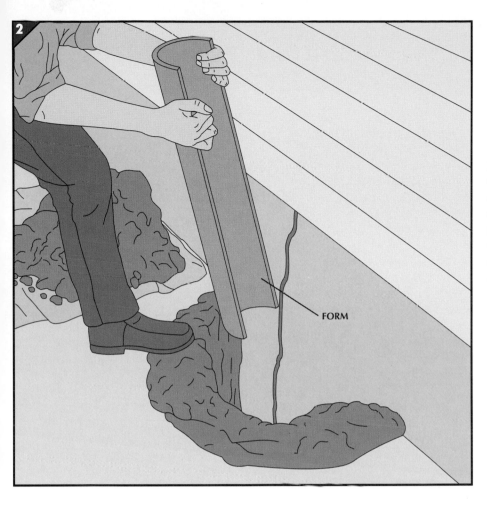

2. Installing the form.

◆ With a compass saw, cut a 9-inch-diameter cylindrical cardboard form for concrete 1 inch longer than the hole depth, then cut it in half lengthwise.

◆ Insert the form in the hole *(left)*, centering it around the crack with its edges flush against the wall. If necessary, remove the form and trim it to fit.

FORM

3. Pouring the bentonite dam.

◆ With the form in place, backfill around it with the excavated soil. Tamp the soil down with a 2-by-4.

◆ Pour granular bentonite into the form, tapping on the top of the form periodically to settle the material.

◆ When the form is full, cover it with a thin layer of soil.

◆ Let the bentonite sit for three months, then use a shovel to remove any soil and bentonite that remains above the surface. Level the ground and cover it with sod.

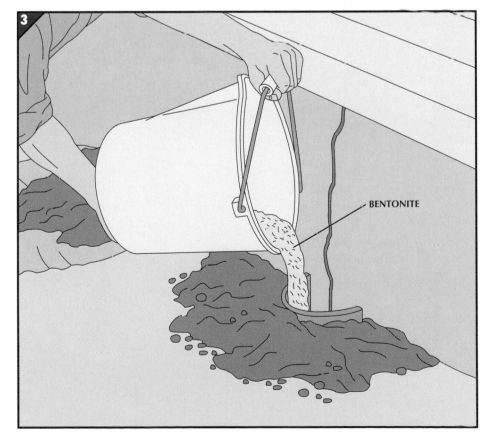

BENTONITE

Expelling Water with a Sump Pump

A sump pump may be the only practical remedy for some wet basements, particularly those where water is forced up through the floor by a fluctuating water table or during severe storms. But a sump pump is also good insurance against water damage from burst pipes or backed-up drains. Stationed in a pit—or sump—in the lowest part of the basement, the pump starts automatically when the water level in the pit rises above a certain point, then switches off once the water has been removed.

Preparing the Pit: In most cases, you will need to break through your basement's concrete floor with a jackhammer. Unless you are comfortable using this tool, you may want to hire a professional.

Depending on local plumbing codes, the pit will be lined with tile, concrete, steel, or plastic. It requires a solid bottom to keep mud from getting into the pump; also needed is a cover to keep out debris and prevent anyone from accidentally stepping into the hole. A supplier can help you choose the right sump liner and accessories.

The discharge line and outlet must also meet local code. Most communities do not allow the water to be pumped into the sewer; but you may be able to pipe it to the storm-drain system or pump it away from the house to drain into the soil.

Wiring the Pump: A sump pump should be wired to a dedicated, unswitched outlet located 4 feet above the pit. Your house's electrical system must be adequate for the job. Unless you are skilled in working with electrical systems, have an electrician wire the pump.

 TOOLS

Screwdriver
Maul
Cold chisel

Jackhammer
Shovel
Mason's trowel
Circular saw
Saber saw

 **MATERIALS**

Pit liner
Gravel
Premixed
  mortar
Discharge pipe,
  coupling,
  elbow,
  threaded
  adapter
Check valve

Pipe-joining
  materials
Flexible adapter
Hose clamps
Hydraulic
  cement
$\frac{3}{4}$" plywood
Galvanized
  wood screws
  ($1\frac{1}{4}$" No. 8)

 **SAFETY TIPS**

Wear a dust mask, hearing protection, goggles, and steel-toed safety boots when operating a jackhammer.

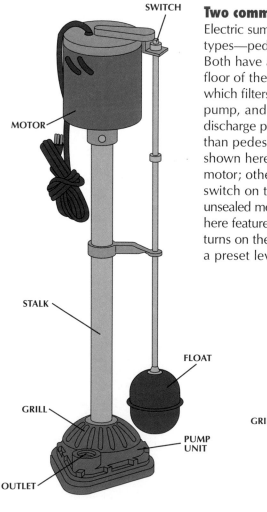

Two common pumps.

Electric sump pumps are available in two basic types—pedestal *(left)* and submersible *(right)*. Both have a rotary pump unit that sits on the floor of the sump. Water enters through a grill, which filters out objects that could damage the pump, and exits from an outlet attached to a discharge pipe. Submersible pumps are quieter than pedestal models. The submersible pump shown here is controlled by a switch inside the motor; other models have an external float switch on the side. Pedestal pumps have an unsealed motor atop a long stalk. The type shown here features a float connected to a switch that turns on the motor when the water rises above a preset level.

SWITCH

MOTOR

STALK

FLOAT

GRILL

PUMP UNIT

OUTLET

PEDESTAL PUMP

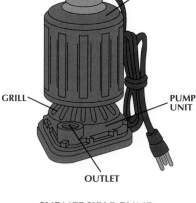

MOTOR

GRILL

PUMP UNIT

OUTLET

SUBMERSIBLE PUMP

INSTALLING A SUMP PUMP

1. Digging the sump.

Locate the sump at the lowest point on the basement floor—typically where water collects—and, if possible, close to a wall and out of the way.

◆ Mark a circle on the floor 3 inches larger in diameter than the sump liner. To do so, tie a piece of chalk to a string, and cut the string $1\frac{1}{2}$ inches longer than the radius of the sump liner. Hold the end of the string where you will locate the center of the circle, and draw the circle with the chalk.

◆ With a jackhammer, chip through the floor within the outline *(left)*. Finish cutting the concrete to the edges of the circle with a cold chisel and maul.

◆ Dig the sump with a shovel or a posthole digger so the hole is about 2 inches deeper than the height of the liner.

◆ For the discharge pipe *(page 52)*, cut a hole 3 inches in diameter through the basement wall about 10 inches below ground level. If the wall is concrete, use the jackhammer or a demolition hammer, which is lighter; if it's made of concrete block, use the cold chisel and maul.

2. Lining the hole.

◆ Place a 1-inch bed of gravel at the bottom of the sump.

◆ Slide the liner into the sump *(right)*; if necessary, remove the cylinder and adjust the gravel so the top of the liner sits just below the floor. Pack soil down around the outside of the liner to a level 1 inch below the floor.

◆ Mix some mortar and pack it over the soil; then, with a mason's trowel, smooth the mortar and slope it from the edge of the floor to the rim of the liner.

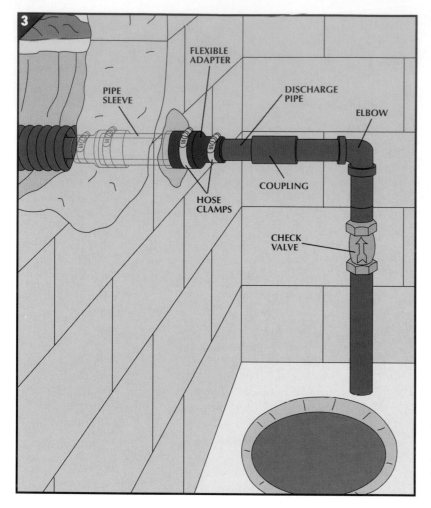

PIPE SLEEVE

FLEXIBLE ADAPTER

DISCHARGE PIPE

ELBOW

COUPLING

HOSE CLAMPS

CHECK VALVE

3. Installing the discharge pipe.

◆ To drain the water into the yard, prepare a ditch like the one on page 36 at the hole you cut through the wall. To direct the water into a storm drain, prepare a similar ditch connecting the line to a drain, but use unperforated drain tile and do not add gravel.

◆ Make a pipe sleeve from a $2\frac{1}{2}$-inch pipe about 4 inches longer than the thickness of the wall. Slide the sleeve to the middle of a 2-foot length of $1\frac{1}{4}$-inch discharge pipe, and secure it there with a flexible adapter—available at plumbing supply stores—on each end. Tighten the hose clamps on the adapters.

◆ Slide the assembly through the wall until the sleeve is positioned in the hole.

◆ Slide the drain tile over the pipe outside and fit it against the house.

◆ With a coupling, extend the discharge pipe to a point about 3 inches past the center of the pit. If the pipe run exceeds 4 feet, strap it to the ceiling joists for support.

◆ Attach an elbow, then a short pipe length, and install a check valve—its arrow pointed away from the pump—to prevent backflow.

◆ Extend the pipe vertically to a point a few inches above the top of the pit.

◆ Pack hydraulic cement into the space between the sleeve and the wall, then backfill the trench.

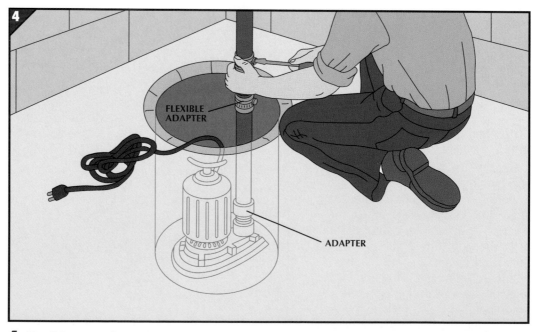

FLEXIBLE ADAPTER

ADAPTER

4. Hooking up the pump.

◆ Attach a threaded adapter onto a length of discharge pipe long enough to extend from the pump outlet to a few inches below the end of the pipe you installed in Step 3. Screw the adapter to the pump outlet.

◆ Lower the pump into the sump and join the pipe ends with a flexible adapter *(above)*, which will make it easy to remove the pump for service. If your sump liner did not come with a cover, make one *(Step 5)*.

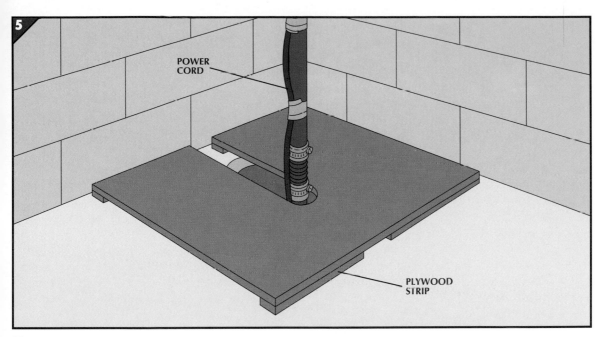

POWER
CORD

PLYWOOD
STRIP

5. Making the cover.

◆ Cut a piece of $\frac{3}{4}$-inch plywood so it extends about 6 inches beyond the rim of the sump.
◆ With a saber saw or compass saw, cut a slot in the cover for the discharge pipe.
◆ With $1\frac{1}{4}$-inch galvanized No. 8 wood screws,

fasten strips of plywood along two opposite sides of the cover to raise it off the floor and allow water to reach the sump.
◆ Tape the pump's power cord to the discharge pipe, then set the cover in place *(above)*.
◆ Have an electrician wire the pump.

A COMPLETE DRAINAGE SYSTEM

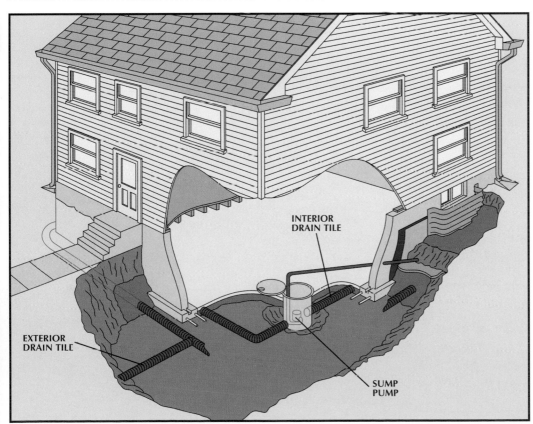

INTERIOR
DRAIN TILE

EXTERIOR
DRAIN TILE

SUMP
PUMP

Making a basement dry.

The scheme shown at left is designed to keep a basement dry at all times. The exterior drain-tile system prevents water buildup around the foundation by directing water away from the house. It can also be set up to empty into the sump inside the house. The interior drain-tile system diverts water under the floor directly into the sump.

Consult a drainage professional to determine whether this approach is practical for your situation. It's costly—so get an estimate for the work.

Attic venting is a crucial part of a home's heating and cooling systems. An unventilated attic can result in problems year-round, even if it is insulated from the rest of the house. At the peak of summer, attic temperatures can reach 150°F, keeping the rest of the house hot long after sundown and putting a heavy and expensive load on air conditioners. In winter, enough heat can accumulate in an attic to melt snow on the roof. The resulting water that runs down the roof can freeze at the eaves and create ice dams.

A steady flow of air through the attic, let in by soffit vents and expelled through roof vents, solves both problems at once—removing hot air in summer and keeping attic air cold and dry in winter.

Soffits and Roof Vents: Openings in the soffits let air enter the bottom of the attic and rise, carrying heat up to be expelled through vents in the gables *(pages 57-59)*, the roof ridge or cupola *(page 63)*, or the roof itself *(pages 60-62)*.

Roof and gable vents are easy to put in, but ridge and cupola vents are best installed by a roofer. When climbing a ladder, use it safely *(page 28)*.

Ventilation Requirements: For every 300 square feet of roof area, you typically need 1 square foot of vent opening—ideally one-half taken up by soffits. If the openings are screened to keep out insects and vermin, the requirement can triple. Your vent supplier can help you determine your needs.

 TOOLS

Tape measure
Chalk line
Compass
Hammer
Utility knife
Wood chisel
Pry bar
Electric drill and
    hole saw
Saber saw
Putty knife
Caulking gun

 **MATERIALS**

2 x 4s
Soffit vents
Roof vents
Gable vents
Common nails ($3\frac{1}{2}$")
Galvanized common
    nails ($1\frac{1}{2}$")
Roofing nails ($1\frac{1}{2}$")
Galvanized wood
    screws ($\frac{3}{4}$" No. 8)
Silicone caulk
Roofing cement

SAFETY TIPS

Wear safety glasses when using power tools or hammering; don a hard hat when working in an unfinished attic.

A range of vents.

Although no one house would have all the vent openings shown at right, the illustration shows typical locations of the vents described on the following pages. Soffit vents fit into the panels, or soffits, that run along the underside of the eaves. They are available in separate units or long strips *(inset, top)*, or the soffit itself may be fully vented *(inset, bottom)*. Gable vents, whether rectangular or triangular, are installed in a gable wall near the roof peak. Roof vents are set into the roof between rafters. Cupola and ridge vents are set into the roof at its highest point, where the rafters meet the ridge beam.

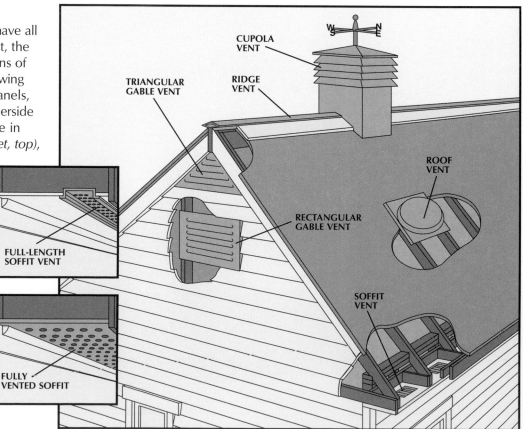

A FULL-LENGTH SOFFIT VENT

CHALK LINE

1. Marking the vent position.
◆ At each end of the soffit, make a mark about 3 inches from the eaves. Tack a nail into the soffit at each mark.
◆ Snap a chalk line between the two nails *(above)*, defining the outside edge of the vent opening.
◆ Measure the width of the soffit vent, and snap a second chalk line on the soffit to mark the vent's inside edge.

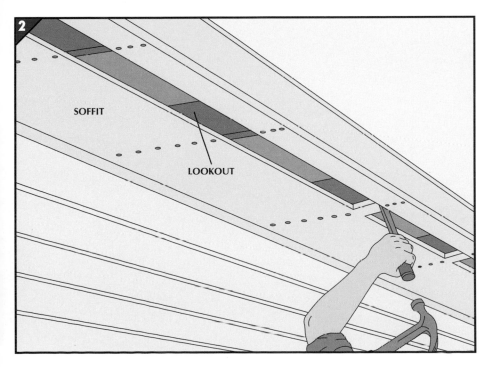

SOFFIT

LOOKOUT

2. Cutting the vent opening.
◆ Between each pair of lookouts—the boards to which the soffit is nailed—drill a $\frac{1}{2}$-inch access hole through the soffit between the chalk lines. Then, with a saber saw, cut out sections of soffit between the lines and lookouts.
◆ To remove the strips of soffit nailed to the lookouts, cut into each piece along the chalk lines with a chisel and pry the strip free *(left)*.
◆ Slip the sections of soffit vent into the opening and nail them to the lookouts with $1\frac{1}{2}$-inch galvanized common nails. Trim the lookouts with the chisel as necessary to ensure a snug fit.

55

ACCESS
HOLE

LOOKOUT

Individual soffit vents.

◆ To install rectangular vents, make a cardboard template matching the vent.
◆ For each vent opening, position the template on the soffit between two lookouts and outline the template.
◆ Drill a $\frac{1}{2}$-inch access hole at each corner of the outline, then cut out the opening with a saber saw *(left)*.
◆ Fasten the vents to the soffit with $\frac{3}{4}$-inch No. 8 galvanized wood screws.

For round vents *(photograph)*, use an electric drill with a hole saw to drill a hole of the appropriate diameter through the soffit; then, snap the vent in place.

Installing a fully vented soffit.

◆ With a saber saw, cut access holes through the soffit between each pair of lookouts.
◆ Pry the soffit from the lookouts *(right)*. To do so, free the outside edge of the soffit first, pivot it below the fascia board, then pull the soffit section off the molding at the wall.
◆ Replace the section with a fully vented soffit, nailing each section to the lookouts.

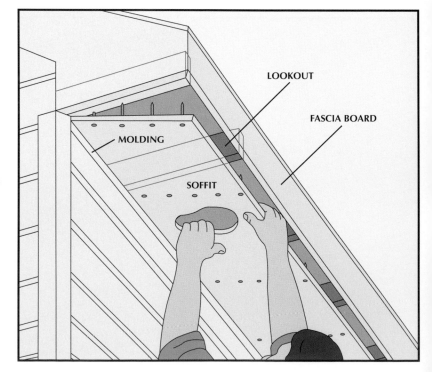

LOOKOUT

FASCIA BOARD

MOLDING

SOFFIT

A RECTANGULAR GABLE VENT

1. Cutting the vent opening.

Locate the vent as close as possible to the roof peak, leaving enough space above the opening for the header you will install in Step 2.

◆ Working inside, outline a rectangle on the gable wall $\frac{1}{4}$ inch larger than the vent. Mark any studs you will have to cut 1$\frac{1}{2}$ inches above and below the outline.

◆ At each corner of the outline, drill a $\frac{1}{2}$-inch access hole through the wall *(left)*; then, with a saber saw, cut the vent opening, sawing through the wall and any studs.

2. Framing the opening.

◆ Cut two 2-by-4 headers to fit between the studs on each side of the vent opening.

◆ Holding the header in position against the cut stud, nail its ends to the studs adjacent to the opening with 3$\frac{1}{2}$-inch common nails *(right)*, then fasten the header to the cut stud.

3. Putting in the vent.

◆ Working outside, apply silicone caulk to the outer flange of the vent and set it into the opening with its louvers facing down.

◆ With a helper outside holding the vent in place, work inside to fasten the vent to the headers with 1½-inch galvanized common nails *(above)*.

◆ If there are nail holes in the outer flange, nail the vent in place *(inset)*.

◆ Caulk the outer edge of the flange, and fill any gaps between the vent flange and the siding with caulk.

A TRIANGULAR GABLE VENT

1. Cutting the vent opening.

◆ Buy a triangular vent that matches the pitch of the roof, or one that can be adjusted to your pitch.

◆ Working inside, outline the vent on the gable wall so the peak of the triangle is just below the bottom edge of the ridge beam *(right)*. Mark any studs you will have to cut 1½ inches below the outline.

◆ At each corner of the triangle, drill a ½-inch hole through the wall; then, with a saber saw, cut the vent opening, sawing through the wall and studs.

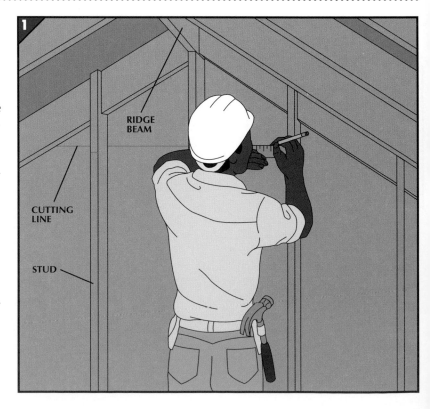

RIDGE BEAM

CUTTING LINE

STUD

2. Fitting in headers.

◆ Cut a 2-by-4 header to fit between the studs on each side of the vent opening, beveling both ends to match the roof slope.

◆ With $3\frac{1}{2}$-inch common nails, fasten the header to the rafters adjacent to the opening and to the cut studs under it.

◆ Cut two more 2-by-4s to fit along the rafters between the ridge beam and the header. Bevel both ends and trim the top corner of each board to sit flush against the ridge beam.

◆ Nail the 2-by-4s to the rafters *(left)*.

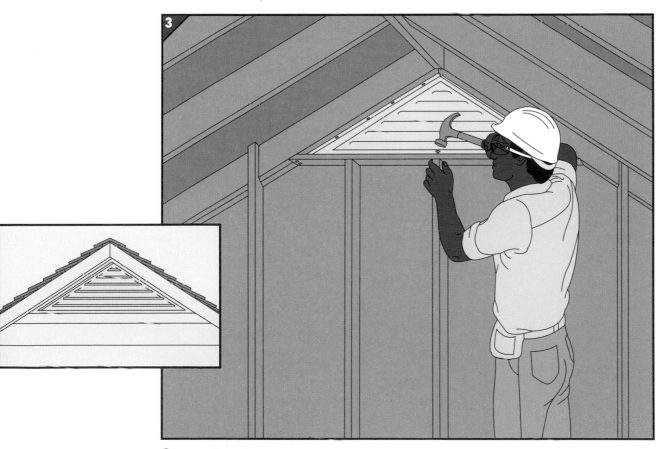

3. Securing the vent.

◆ Outside, apply silicone caulk to the outer vent flange and fit it into position in the opening.

◆ If the outer flange has nail holes, fasten the flange to the wall with $1\frac{1}{2}$-inch galvanized common nails.

◆ Apply caulk all around the edge of the outer flange.

◆ Inside the attic, nail the inner vent flange to the header and 2-by-4s with $1\frac{1}{2}$-inch galvanized nails *(above)*.

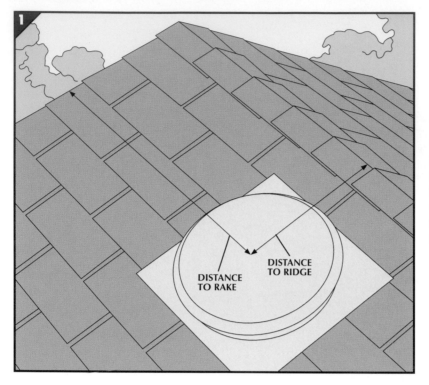

1. Positioning the vent.

◆ Set the vent assembly at the desired position on the roof at least 12 inches from the ridge. If you are installing more than one vent, space them evenly.

◆ For each vent, measure the distances from the center of the assembly to the ridge and to the nearest rake, subtracting the width of any overhang *(left)*.

2. Centering the vent.

◆ Working inside the attic, use the measurements from Step 1 to locate the center of the vent on the sheathing.

◆ Adjust the vent-to-rake measurement to center the vent between two rafters, then mark the center point by driving a nail through the roof *(right)*.

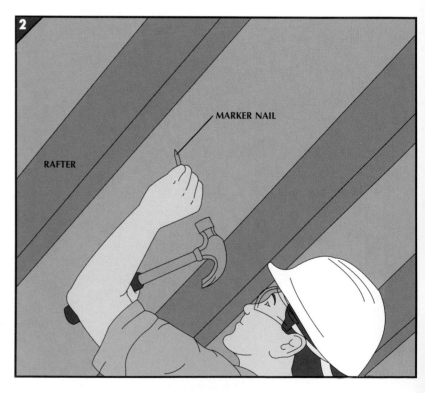

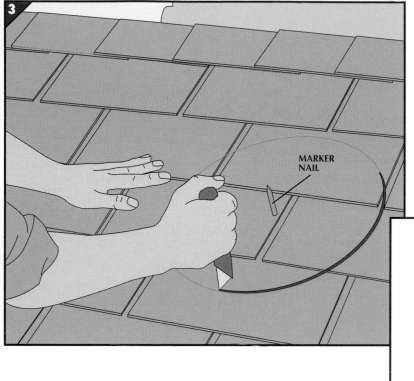

3. An opening for the vent base.
◆ Measure the diameter of the base of the vent housing *(inset)*.
◆ Using the marker nail as a center point, scribe a circle of the measured diameter on the roof with a compass.
◆ With a utility knife, cut out the shingles and roofing felt within the circle, exposing sheathing. Pry out any nails.

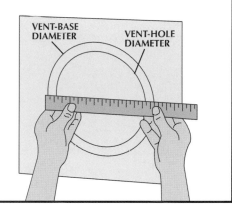

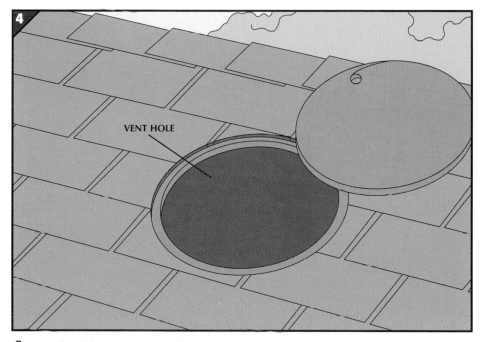

4. Cutting the vent opening.
◆ Measure the diameter of the vent hole and mark a matching circle on the sheathing from the same center point.

◆ Drill an access hole within the vent-hole circle, then cut out the sheathing within the circle with a saber saw or compass saw *(above)*.

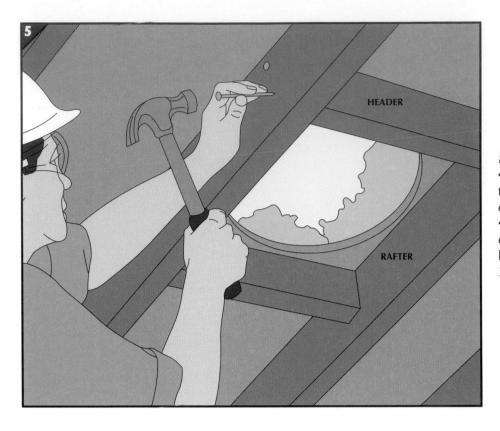

HEADER

RAFTER

5. Attaching headers.

◆ Cut two 2-by-4 headers to fit between the rafters on each side of the vent hole.

◆ Above and below the vent opening, fasten the headers between the rafters with $3\frac{1}{2}$-inch common nails *(left)*.

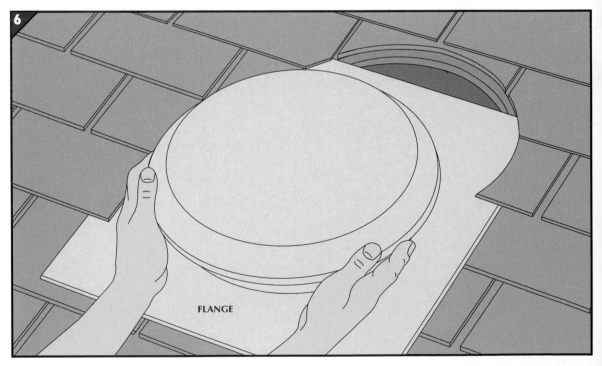

FLANGE

6. Installing the vent.

◆ On the roof, slide the vent assembly into position up under the cut shingles surrounding the vent opening. If there are nails in the way, remove them with a pry bar. Have a helper inside confirm that the vent is centered over the opening.

◆ Apply roofing cement under the downroof edge of the flange, then fasten the vent to the roof with $1\frac{1}{2}$-inch roofing nails driven at the corners of the flange and the middle of each side. To access the flange on the uproof side of the opening, pull the shingles back.

◆ Cover exposed nailheads with roofing cement.

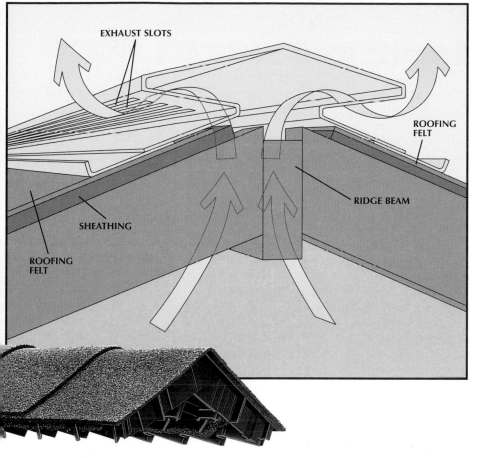

EXHAUST SLOTS

ROOFING FELT

SHEATHING

ROOFING FELT

RIDGE BEAM

A ridge vent.

When combined with soffit vents, a ridge vent is the most efficient way to air out an attic. Installed over a continuous opening cut through the roof along the peak, it lets hot air from the attic leave through exhaust slots.

To install the type shown at left, the roofing material is removed along the ridge as well as 1 inch of sheathing on each side of the ridge beam. The vent is secured with $1\frac{1}{2}$-inch roofing nails, then the roofing material is replaced.

Some ridge vents are made of plastic and come already covered with shingles to match the roof *(photograph)*.

A cupola vent.

Installed at the ridge, a cupola vent lends a stately appearance to a house. Like a ridge vent, it functions best in combination with soffit venting. For some installations it may be necessary to remove a section of ridge beam and frame the opening with headers; the cupola is then secured to the headers and the rafters at the sides of the opening. A flange on the bottom of the cupola fits under the surrounding shingles and is sealed with roofing cement.

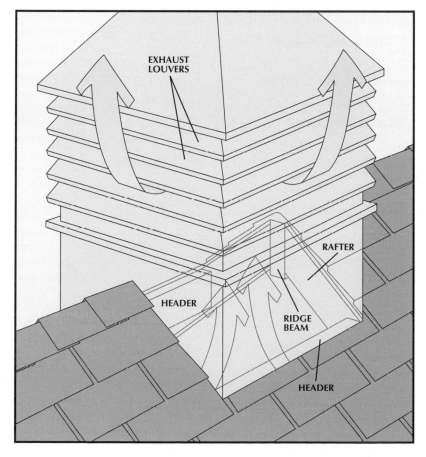

EXHAUST LOUVERS

RAFTER

HEADER

RIDGE BEAM

HEADER

Shielding Against Heat and Cold

Your closest ally in keeping a home warm in winter and cool in summer is adequate insulation. This chapter shows how to evaluate your needs and apply insulation where it will do the most good—in the attic, the exterior walls, and the basement or crawl space. These pages also explain how to install storm windows and doors to keep out the cold, and awnings to block the summer sun.

Wrapping insulation around a duct →

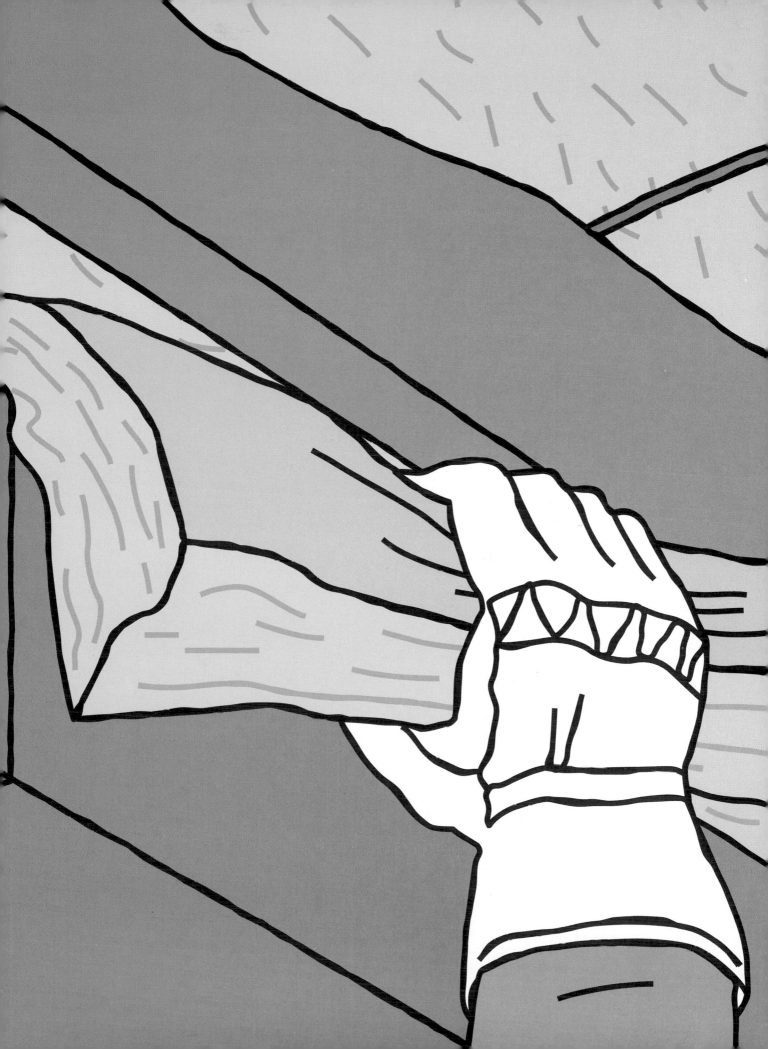

Houses come in a wide variety of shapes and sizes, but most homes incorporate some of the elements in the illustration at right. The diagram shows the spaces that typically require insulation; finished walls have been removed for clarity.

Use the drawing as a guide, and make a list of the areas in your home that need insulation. The principle is simple: Insulate any surface separating living spaces from unheated areas.

Insulation prevents heat from escaping from your house in winter, but it also keeps the house cooler in summer. A well-insulated attic, for example, shields living areas from the heat of the sun. When bolstered by the weatherproofing measures described in Chapter 1, and the practices for providing shade on pages 106 to 109, insulation will make the interior of a house noticeably cooler than the outside temperature in summer—even without air-conditioning.

Attics and Ceilings: Because the attic is potentially the greatest source of heat exchange in a house, deal with it first *(pages 74-84)*. For an unfinished attic, you need only insulate the floor; finished attics call for a bit more work. Cathedral ceilings are difficult to access and don't offer much space for insulation. For such a ceiling, it's best to have a professional do the job.

Walls: All exterior walls should be insulated, including any wall of a split-level home that rises above an adjacent roof. It's simplest to install insulation in a wall during its construction, but even if a wall is finished, there are a number of ways to insulate it without removing the wall covering *(pages 85-89)*.

Cellars and Crawl Spaces: If your house has an unheated cellar or crawl space, the floor directly above it—as well as pipes and ducts running through it—should be insulated *(pages 90-93)*. For a heated cellar, crawl space, or finished basement, use the methods on pages 94 to 98.

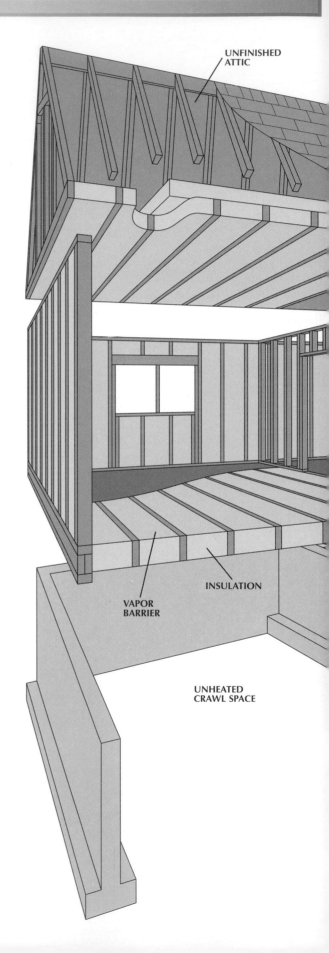

UNFINISHED ATTIC

INSULATION

VAPOR BARRIER

UNHEATED CRAWL SPACE

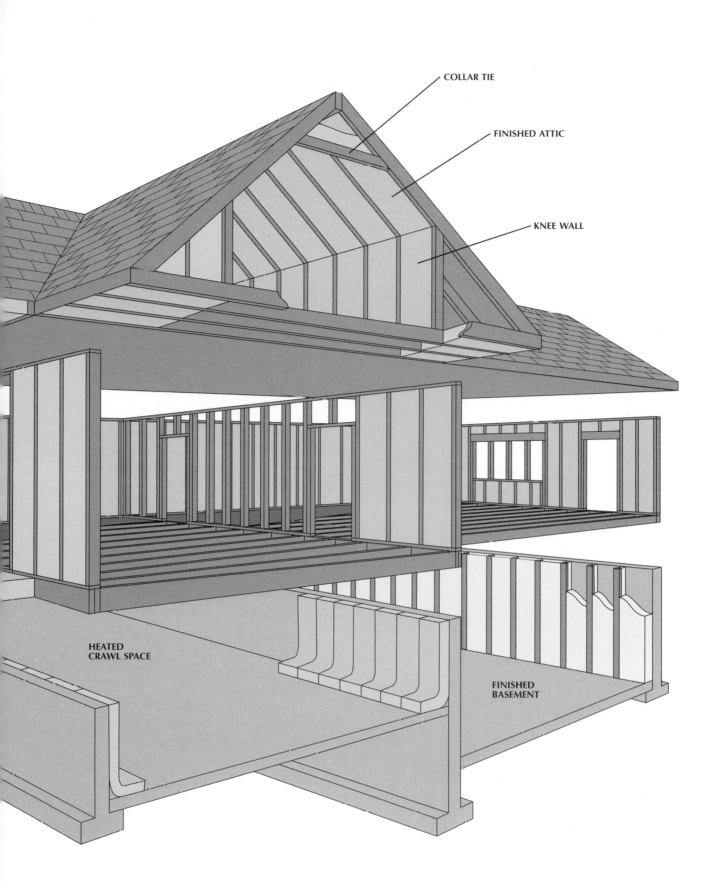

COLLAR TIE

FINISHED ATTIC

KNEE WALL

HEATED
CRAWL SPACE

FINISHED
BASEMENT

Checking for Adequate Insulation

Before you can estimate your insulation needs, you must determine what kind and how much the house already has. The most common types are listed on page 72.

A good place to begin an insulation audit is an unfinished area such as the attic, basement, crawl space, or garage. Insulation here will be visible between joists, beams, and studs; the thickness of the material can be measured with a ruler.

Looking Behind Walls: Insulation inside finished walls can often be checked through existing openings such as light switches and receptacles *(below)*. When a wall has no such apertures, remove the louvers of forced-air ducts and examine the edge of the duct; or, pry off a section of baseboard and drill a small peephole through the exposed wall.

If the insulation has a vapor barrier —a lining of kraft paper, plastic, or aluminum foil to keep moisture from condensing on interior walls—patch any holes you make in it with duct tape, and plastic sheeting if necessary, before resealing the wall.

Evaluating Your Needs: Plan on replacing insulation that has been damaged by moisture, as well as any flammable materials like sawdust or rags used as insulation.

Once you know the type of insulation you have and how thick it is, estimate its approximate R-value—or insulating capacity—by multiplying the thickness in inches by the R-value per inch in the chart on page 72. Then refer to the map *(page 70)* and chart *(page 71)* to determine the optimum R-values for different parts of the house in your region.

 TOOLS

Tape measure   Handsaw
Screwdriver   Electric drill
Pry bars

 **MATERIALS**

Wire
Masking tape
Plastic sheeting
Dowel ($\frac{1}{2}$")

 **SAFETY TIPS**

Wear a dust mask, a long-sleeved shirt, and gloves when handling fiberglass insulation.

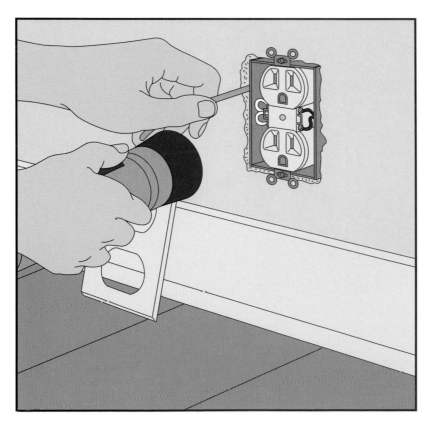

Checking wall insulation at an outlet.
◆ Shut off power to the outlet at the service panel.
◆ Remove the outlet's cover plate and look into the gap between the electrical box and the plaster or wallboard, lighting the opening with a flashlight. If there is a vapor barrier just inside the opening, you probably have blanket or batt-type insulation. Otherwise, the insulation is likely loose fill or foamed-in-place. Identify the type of loose fill by inserting a hooked length of stiff wire into the gap and pulling out a sample *(left)*.

For the loose-fill type, check whether it has settled in the wall, leaving gaps near the ceiling. Place the palm of your hand against the wall every 3 feet, starting at the baseboard and working toward the ceiling. When the temperature outside is cold and you feel the wall become noticeably cooler as your hand climbs the wall, the fill has settled; during hot weather, the wall will feel warmer. When either is the case, refill the cavity *(pages 86-88)*.

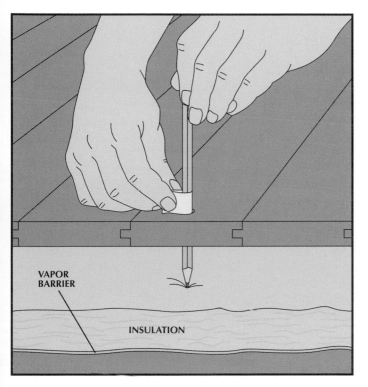

VAPOR
BARRIER

INSULATION

Measuring the insulation under a floor.

If your attic flooring consists of straightedged boards nailed down, pull up a board with a pair of pry bars and inspect the insulation.

◆ Where the floorboards are tongue-and-groove, drill a $\frac{1}{2}$-inch hole through a board between two joists.

◆ Insert a sharpened pencil into the hole and when you feel resistance as the pencil contacts the insulation, wrap a strip of tape around the pencil at floor level *(left)*.

◆ Push the pencil through the insulation so the point reaches the vapor barrier and wrap another tape strip around the pencil.

◆ Measure the distance between the strips to determine the thickness of the insulation.

◆ To identify the insulating material, remove a piece with a hooked wire.

◆ Plug the hole in the floorboard by gluing in a dowel.

TESTING INSULATION WITH INFRARED SCANNING

A visual inspection is one way to assess a home's insulation, but a more precise technique called infrared scanning can pinpoint areas where heat is escaping.

Readings are usually taken when there is a 25°F to 30°F difference between inside and outside temperatures. The various temperature levels appear on an infrared image as colors: warm colors such as red and brown indicate greater heat loss than cool colors like green and blue. The image at left, for example, shows that heat is escaping from the wall above the two windows.

After you've identified areas of your house that need more insulation, you can check which ones are losing the most heat and attend to them first. Or, if you have contractors install the insulation, you can take a reading afterward to assess the work. To find this service in the Yellow Pages, look under "Infrared Inspection Services" or "Thermography—Inspection Services."

Deciding How Much to Add

There is no simple formula for determining the precise amount of insulation you need. Variations in climate, fuel costs, and the efficiency of a heating system all figure in the equation. Even the type and site of a house can make a difference. A one-story house requires more insulation than a two-story one with the same floor space because its roof is larger. The same is true of a house that isn't sheltered—it tends to be chilled by winds.

Climate Zones: The map below, used to establish minimum R-values for insulation in different regions, divides the United States into eight climate zones. A number of different factors are used to define the zones, but the most important is the "degree-day"—the difference between the average temperature of a single day and 65°F. On a day with an average temperature of 42°F, for example, the degree-day reading is 23 (or 65 less 42). When totaled for an entire year, degree days range from less than 2,500 in the South to more than 10,000 in parts of Alaska. The insulation requirement rises with the total. Another factor is the lowest temperature that can be expected during the winter. This ranges from 40°F in Florida to -50°F in parts of Alaska.

Insulating to Improve Cooling: Insulation needs are influenced by how hot it gets in your area. Cooling hours—the total number of hours in a year above 78°F, when air conditioners are usually in operation—can top 1,500 in some regions. As in winter, these temperature extremes call for insulation—in this case, to minimize air-conditioning costs. For example, a house in Miami, situated in a warm climate, needs more insulation than one in San Francisco, whose climate is temperate.

Finding your climate zone.
This map depicts the eight climate zones, ranging from subtropical Florida, where heating costs are negligible but air-conditioning costs are high, to parts of Maine and the Midwest where winter temperatures can drop to -30°F or colder. Most of Hawaii is in Zone 1, while Alaska is in Zone 8. For the amount of insulation suggested for each zone, see the chart opposite.

FIND THE R-VALUES OF YOUR ZONE

Zone	Ceilings directly below roof or unheated attic		Exterior walls	Floors above unheated basement or crawl spaces	Walls of heated crawl spaces
	Fossil fuel	Electric heat			
1	R-19	R-30	R-11	R-11	R-11
2	R-30	R-30	R-11	R-11	R-19
3	R-30	R-38	R-11	R-19	R-19
4	R-30	R-38	R-11	R-19	R-19
5	R-38	R-38	R-11	R-19	R-19
6	R-38	R-38	R-11	R-19	R-19
7	R-38	R-49	R-11	R-19	R-19
8	R-49	R-49	R-11	R-19	R-19

Insulation R-value standards.

This chart lists minimum acceptable standards for insulation. Since a large part of the cost of insulating is labor, exceeding the standards does not appreciably increase costs.

As you plan your insulation strategy, keep in mind that houses with electric-resistance heating systems require about 25 percent more insulation in the attic. In addition, most houses have walls built with $3\frac{1}{2}$-inch studs, so the amount of insulation you can add is limited unless you want to install rigid panels on the exterior of the house. Insulating floors over an unheated basement beyond the thickness of the joists is usually not worth the extra effort. Similarly, insulating heated crawl spaces beyond R-19 is not cost effective.

Choosing the Right Materials

The type of insulation you choose will depend on your climate, your budget, and the part of the house you are insulating. The first consideration is maximizing the R-value most economically. Other factors include ease of installation, and fire and moisture resistance.

All types of insulation, whether in the form of batts or blankets, loose fill, or foam, work by trapping air in millions of tiny pockets. Since air is a very poor conductor, it resists the flow of heat.

Batts or Blankets: Fiberglass is reasonably priced, fire resistant, and nonabsorbent. Rock wool, which is spun from molten limestone, has similar characteristics.

A batt of either material is about 99 percent air and 1 percent spun fiber and phenolic binder.

Loose Fill: Cellulose insulation, derived from newspaper and wood wastes, is usually applied as loose fill. It has a higher R-value than fiberglass or rock wool, but must be treated with fire retardants, which can lose their effectiveness over time. Loose fill may also be made of vermiculite (a form of mica) or perlite (volcanic ash). To prevent loose fill from settling in walls, apply it to the density recommended by the manufacturer.

Foam: One type of foam insulation, polystyrene, comes in rigid boards or sheets and is widely used to insulate masonry walls and basements. Another, called foamed-in-place, consists of a plastic foam that flows around obstructions to fill a space completely, then hardens.

Stopping Condensation: By blocking heat flow, insulation solves one problem, but creates another—condensation. When temperature differences between inside and outside wall surfaces increase, and vapor passes through the insulation, moisture condenses on the colder wall. This reduces the effectiveness of fibrous insulation, and the damage to paint and wood can be significant. The solution is a vapor barrier *(opposite)*.

TYPES OF INSULATION

Material	Approximate R-value per inch of thickness	Common Forms	Advantages	Disadvantages
Fiberglass	3.1-3.7 (blankets, batts) 2.9-3.7 (loose fill)	Blankets, batts, loose fill	Inexpensive, fire resistant	Particles irritate skin and lungs during installation
Rock wool	3.1-3.7 (blankets, batts) 2.9-3.7 (loose fill)	Blankets, batts, loose fill	Inexpensive, fire resistant	Particles irritate skin and lungs during installation
Cellulose	3.1-3.7	Loose fill	Easy to blow in; nonirritating	Absorbs moisture; fire retardants can corrode metal; may settle
Vermiculite and perlite	2.1-2.3 (vermiculite) 2.7 (perlite)	Loose fill	Fire resistant; easily poured into wall cavities	Low R-value; may settle; expensive in some regions
Polystyrene	4.4-5.0 (extruded type); 3.8-5.0 (expanded type)	Rigid boards	Extruded type is moisture resistant	Flammable; gives off toxic fumes when burning. Expanded type not moisture resistant
Polyurethane	5.8-6.2	Foamed-in-place	Expands to fill small cracks; moisture resistant	Requires professional installation; gives off toxic fumes when burning

A FORM FOR EVERY PURPOSE

Insulation comes in many forms, but the four shown here are the most common. Rigid boards of extruded polystyrene *(top)*, due to their high resistance to moisture, are especially good for insulating basements. However, they are flammable and must be covered with at least $\frac{1}{2}$ inch of gypsum wallboard for fire protection. Fiberglass batts *(second from top)*—available in thicknesses of $3\frac{1}{2}$ to 7 inches and 8-foot lengths—are designed to fit between 16- or 24-inch stud and joist spacings. For an uninsulated space, buy the type that has a vapor barrier already attached, with flanges for stapling the batt to the framing; buy plain batts to lay over existing insulation for extra R-value. Available in rolls, blankets *(third from top)* are ideal for covering a large space quickly. Like batts, they are available with or without a vapor barrier. Loose fill *(bottom)*, which requires a separate vapor barrier, is easy to spread over open, flat spaces like attic floors; or to blow inside finished walls through access holes.

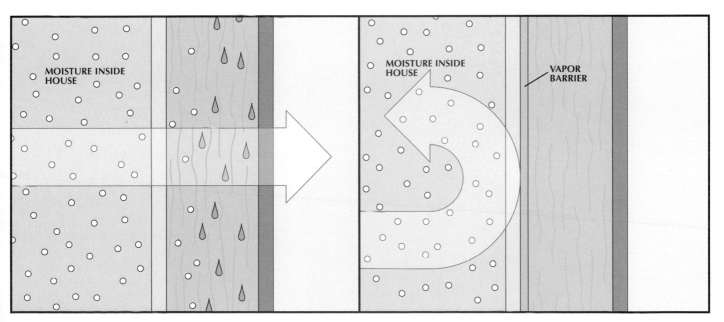

How a vapor barrier works.

In winter, warm humid air passes through insulation without a vapor barrier and condenses when it meets the cold of an exterior wall *(above, left)*. Adding a vapor barrier of kraft paper, heavy polyethylene sheeting, aluminum foil, or waterproof paint prevents moisture from passing beyond the interior surface of the insulation *(above, right)*. Since it never contacts the cold, it cannot condense.

The rule of thumb is to install the vapor barrier on the side of the insulation that is warmer in winter. An exception is the humid Southeast, where the barrier should face the outside. In areas where the average January temperature is 35°F or higher and the number of days the house is cooled greatly exceeds the number of days it is heated, the vapor barrier should be omitted.

The most important part of the house to insulate is the attic—not only does heat escape through it in winter, but heat builds up there in summer. Whether your attic is an unfinished, unheated, unused space without a floor *(page 75)*; an unfinished, unheated, storage area with a floor *(pages 77-78)*; or a finished and heated room *(pages 82-84)*, insulating the house begins here. Include the stairway or access hatch *(pages 79-81)*; in most homes, this opening acts as a gaping hole for heat transfer. However, do not seal your attic space completely; attics need adequate ventilation *(pages 54-63)*.

Preparing an Attic: If your attic has no floor, install temporary flooring (and lighting, if necessary) before insulating. Wire work lights and lay plywood across the joists as a work platform. Don't step on the ceiling below—it may break.

If your attic already has some insulation, and a vapor barrier is required in your area, first ascertain whether or not there is a barrier. If not, remove the old insulation before beginning the job.

Insulation with a Barrier: The most practical insulation materials for the attic are batts or blankets with an attached vapor barrier, which are easy to handle in the confined spaces under the roof. Choose a thickness that will allow you to leave a 1-inch gap between the roof sheathing and the insulation for ventilation. Loose fill can also be applied between the joists, but you'll need to add a separate vapor barrier *(below)*.

If you are laying batts or blankets as an extra layer over existing floor insulation, buy material with no vapor barrier—this will prevent moisture from being trapped between the insulation layers.

TOOLS

Tape measure	Straightedge
Hammer	Hand stapler
Screwdriver	Pry bar
Utility knife	Handsaw
	Circular saw
	Caulking gun

MATERIALS

2 x 4s	Hinges
Plywood flooring	Polyethylene
$\frac{1}{2}$" plywood	sheeting
Common nails (2", 3")	Soffit baffle
Wood screws	Duct tape
($\frac{1}{2}$" No. 8)	Aluminum foil
	Caulk
	Panel adhesive

SAFETY TIPS

Wear gloves, long sleeves, goggles, and a dust mask when installing fiberglass or rock-wool insulation. Add a hard hat when working in an unfinished attic.

Stapling down a vapor barrier.

◆ For loose-fill insulation, buy strips of polyethylene sheeting at least 4 mils thick.

◆ Cut the strips a few inches wider than the joist spacing.

◆ Lay the strips between the joists and staple them every 6 inches to the sides of the joists at the ceiling below, holding the sheeting flat to avoid gaps or bulges *(left)*. Patch any tears with duct tape.

◆ To prevent the insulation from billowing out over the top plate and blocking the soffit vents, install a preformed baffle, available from your insulation supplier, at the eaves between each pair of rafters.

BATTS OR BLANKETS FOR AN UNFINISHED FLOOR

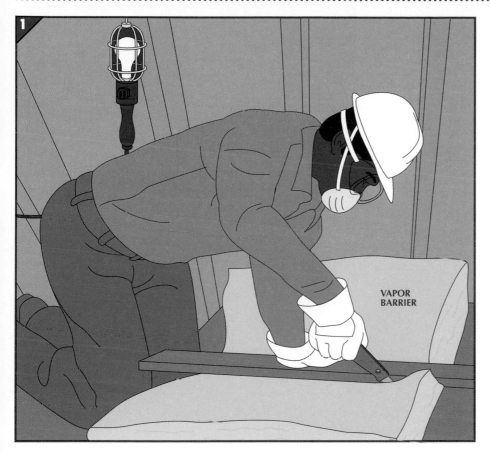

VAPOR BARRIER

1. Cutting the batts or blankets.
With the vapor barrier facing up, lay the insulation on a flat, firm surface. Compress the material by holding a straight board along the cutting line, then slice through it with a utility knife *(left)*.

A HANDY INSULATION CUTTER

Paired with a utility knife, the special knife holder shown here is a handy tool for compressing and slicing insulation at the same time. As you press down on the knife to cut, the curved holder compacts the insulation. Made of springy plastic, the holder accommodates most models of utility knife.

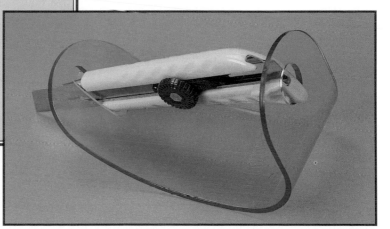

2. Insulating between joists.

◆ Start each row of insulation at one eave, pushing the batt or blanket between the joists with its vapor barrier facing down *(right).* Align the end of the insulation with the outside edge of the top plate *(inset);* do not jam the insulation against the eaves—this will block the airflow.

◆ Once you reach the middle of the attic, finish the row from the opposite eave, butting the ends of the insulation tightly together.

◆ Cut the insulation to fit snugly around obstacles, such as pipes, and slide it under wires. For any electrical fixture that is not marked "IC" (Insulation-Contact Rated), build a plywood box around the fixture to separate it from the insulation by at least 3 inches.

◆ Wrap chimneys with heavy-duty aluminum foil, fastening and sealing the foil with caulk rated for contact with chimneys.

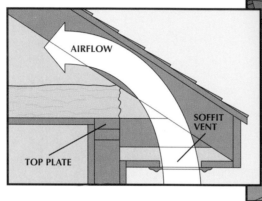

AIRFLOW

SOFFIT VENT

TOP PLATE

INSULATION

AN EXTRA LAYER FOR ADDED PROTECTION

Adding insulation.

◆ To provide a base for new flooring, cut 2-by-4 supports long enough to span from the attic floor to 1 inch above the new insulation and, with 3-inch common nails, fasten them at 2-foot intervals to one side of every other joist.

◆ Top the existing layer of insulation with batts or blankets without vapor barriers, laying them perpendicular to the joists *(left);* or cover it with loose fill.

2 x 4 SUPPORT

INSULATING THE ATTIC CEILING

COLLAR TIE

1. Installing collar ties.
In an unfinished attic with a floor, insulate the ceiling to avoid removing and reinstalling the flooring. Add collar ties if the bottom edge of the boards will provide 6 feet of headroom. Otherwise, insulate the attic using the method on page 78.
◆ For each pair of rafters, cut 2-by-4 collar ties long enough to contact the sheathing on both sides of the roof at a convenient height for laying insulation.
◆ Set up a scaffold, if necessary, by placing plywood across a pair of sawhorses. With a helper holding the boards in place, fasten the ties to the rafters with 3-inch common nails *(left)*.

2. Insulating the ceiling.
◆ Cut lengths of insulation slightly shorter than the collar ties.
◆ Center the insulation between the ties with the vapor barrier facing down and staple the flanges along the sides of the insulation to the bottom edges of the ties at 6-inch intervals.
◆ For adjacent pieces, overlap the flanges to lie flat.
◆ In the same manner, fasten insulation to the rafters from the collar ties down to the floor *(right)*.
◆ At the junction of the collar tie and rafters, seal the seam between lengths of insulation with duct tape, creating a continuous vapor barrier.

3. Insulating the end walls.

◆ With the vapor barrier facing the room, fit batts or blankets between the wall studs. Staple the flanges every 6 inches to the studs.

◆ Trim pieces of insulation, as necessary, to cover the walls completely and fit snugly into small gaps in the framing around windows or louvers without being compressed *(right)*.

TRICKS OF THE TRADE

A Custom Fit for Small Gaps

Attics that are otherwise well insulated can contribute to higher heating bills if the spaces surrounding electric cables, plumbing chases, and other channels from a cold basement or crawl space are left unsealed. Such "chimneys" funnel cold air up to the attic, cooling off the living areas below. Block these openings by stuffing in plastic freezer bags filled with fiberglass insulation; the bag serves as a vapor barrier.

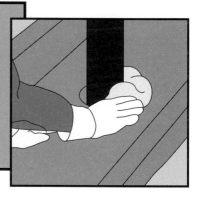

DEALING WITH A LOW CEILING

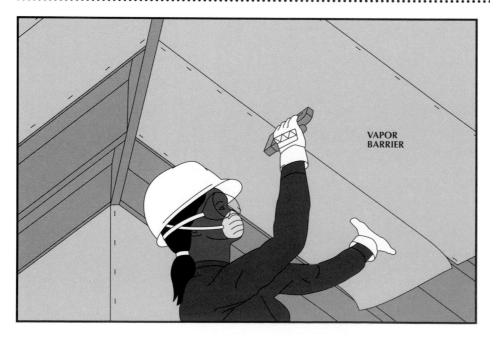

VAPOR BARRIER

Insulating the attic.

◆ Insulate the end walls as shown above.

◆ With the vapor barrier facing down, fit batts or blankets between the rafters.

◆ Staple the flanges along the sides of the insulation to the edges of the rafters at 6-inch intervals *(left)*. At the ridge, butt the end of the batt or blanket tightly against the ridge board.

FILLING THE STAIRS

Insulating treads with loose fill.

◆ If there is a finished ceiling under the stairs, pry off the top tread and pour loose fill into the space *(right)*. Push the insulation down to the bottom of the staircase with a broom handle or long, thin board as you go, filling the space completely. For a long stairway, start pouring insulation at a tread halfway up, then fill in the rest of the cavity from the top.

◆ If the wall studs framing the staircase are exposed and uninsulated, fit batts or blankets between them *(page 83, Step 2)*; if there is a door, glue rigid insulation boards to its back with panel adhesive.

Where there is no finished ceiling below the stairs, cut a piece of $\frac{1}{2}$-inch plywood to cover the underside of the stairs, and staple a 4-mil polyethylene vapor barrier to one side of the plywood. With 2-inch common nails, nail the piece barrier-side up to the bottom edge of the stringers—the boards that run along the sides of the steps. Then insulate as described above.

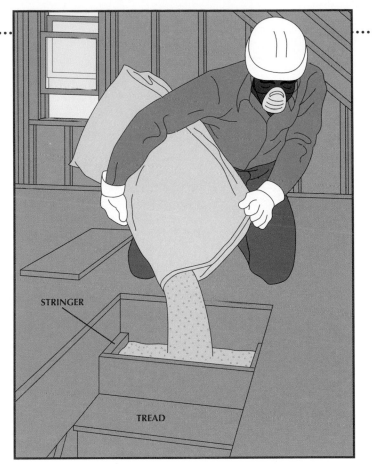

A BOX FOR A HATCHWAY

1. Measuring the stairway depth.

◆ If the hatchway has pull-down steps, lower them. Do not unfold folding-type steps.

◆ Measure the thickness of the stairs to determine how much clearance they need when raised into the attic *(left)*.

PLYWOOD

HEADER

UPRIGHT

JOIST

2. Boxing in the opening.
◆ Remove 10 inches of attic flooring beyond the header at the top of the stairs, and 4 inches beyond the header at the opposite end of the opening.
◆ Cut four 2-by-4 uprights 2 inches longer than the measurement made in Step 1.
◆ Fasten the uprights to the joists at each corner of the opening with 3-inch common nails.
◆ For the sides of the box, attach pieces of $\frac{1}{2}$-inch plywood to the uprights with 2-inch common nails *(left)*.
◆ Replace the flooring across the header at the top of the stairs to serve as a step into the attic; also replace the flooring on the outside of the box at the opposite end.

3. Finishing the box.
◆ Cut two 2-by-4 spacers as long as the height of the box.
◆ On the side of the box where the lid will be attached *(Step 4)*, secure the spacers to the uprights with 3-inch common nails driven through the plywood.
◆ Cut two 2-by-4 lid rests 8 inches longer than the spacers and nail them to the outsides of the spacers *(right)*.

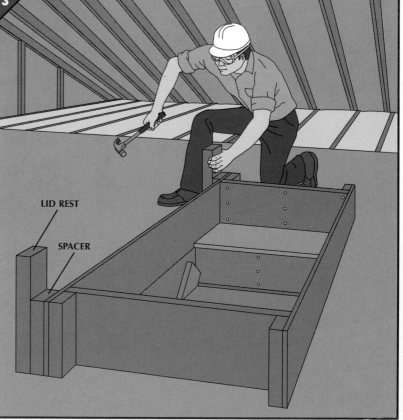

LID REST

SPACER

4. Attaching the lid.

◆ Cover the box with a lid cut from $\frac{1}{2}$-inch plywood. To prevent the lid from warping, fasten a 2-by-4 along one edge with 2-inch nails.

◆ Along the other edge of the lid, attach butt hinges 6 inches from each end with $\frac{1}{2}$-inch No. 8 wood screws *(right)*.

◆ Fasten a handle to the inside of the lid so you can pull it down when leaving the attic.

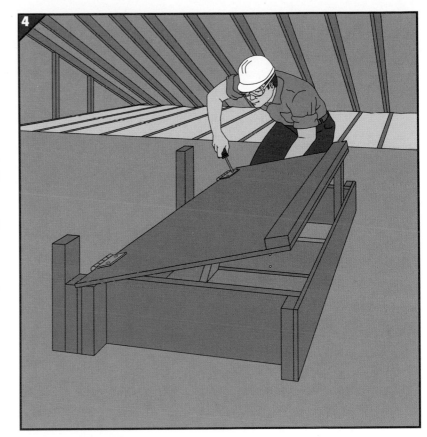

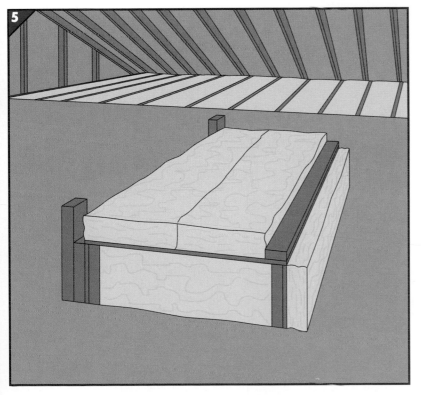

5. Insulating the box.

◆ Cut two batts or blankets to fit snugly against the plywood at the ends of the box.

◆ With the vapor barriers facing the plywood, staple the insulation flanges to the plywood every 6 inches.

◆ Cut two more pieces of insulation for the sides of the box and staple them in place.

◆ Add pieces to cover the lid and staple them—vapor barrier down—to the lid.

The biggest challenge in insulating a finished attic is getting to the places you want to insulate. To access them, you will have to cut holes in the ceiling and side—or knee—walls (*opposite, Step 1*). Once the insulation is put in place, the openings can be closed with removable panels or sealed with wallboard (*page 84*).

Boosting R-Value: Although the knee walls and the flat part of the ceiling can usually be insulated with batts or blankets, loose fill is easier to install in the sloping portion of the ceiling, provided it has sufficient R-value for your region's climate (*opposite, Step 2*). You can boost the rating by substituting rigid polystyrene boards, which have a higher R-value per inch than loose fill. A bit more work is required, however. You'll need to trim the boards to fit between the rafters and slide them into place from the opening in the flat part of the ceiling. The batts insulating the knee walls will hold the boards in place.

Vapor Barriers: To prevent batt or blanket insulation from absorbing moisture, position the vapor barrier against the attic's finished walls and ceiling. If you are installing loose fill, coat the ceiling surface on the interior of the room with a vapor-barrier paint. With rigid polystyrene boards, no vapor barrier is necessary.

 TOOLS

Hammer	Electric drill
Screwdriver	Saber saw
Hand stapler	Circular saw
Utility knife	

 **MATERIALS**

1 x 2s	Insulation (loose fill and
2 x 4s	blankets or batts)
$\frac{1}{2}$" plywood	Wallboard repair materials
Common nails ($2\frac{1}{2}$", $3\frac{1}{2}$")	Turn buttons

 **SAFETY TIPS**

Wear goggles when using power tools or driving nails. When handling insulation, wear long sleeves, gloves, goggles, and a dust mask. Add a hard hat when working in an unfinished part of the attic.

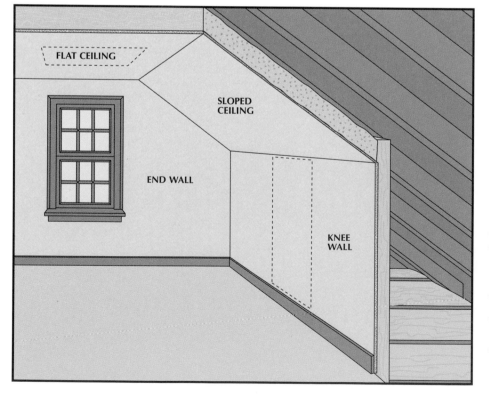

FLAT CEILING

SLOPED CEILING

END WALL

KNEE WALL

A well-insulated attic.

Batts or blankets are fastened to the studs behind the knee walls, and between the floor joists outside the knee walls. Loose fill packs the sloping portion of the ceiling, held there by the top of the knee wall's insulation; in cold areas, R-value may be boosted by filling this slope with rigid polystyrene boards instead. The flat area of the ceiling is insulated with batts or blankets; if the space is too small to maneuver in, loose fill can be blown in to cover the ceiling. The cavity behind the end walls is insulated from outside (*pages 85-89*).

The access holes through the knee wall and ceiling are indicated by the dashed lines. Depending on the size of your attic, several openings may be necessary.

STUD

ACCESS HOLE

1. Cutting the wall and ceiling openings.

◆ Turn off the power to all electrical circuits in the work area.

◆ Drill a $\frac{1}{2}$-inch access hole through the wall; then, with a saber saw or a compass saw, cut across to the nearest wall stud, being careful not to hit any wires. Saw along the framing in a rectangular pattern *(left)* until you return to the access hole and can remove the section of wall.

◆ Cut an opening in the ceiling the same way.

2. Applying the insulation.

◆ In the unfinished part of the attic, put down a piece of plywood as a working platform and lay batts or blankets between the floor joists *(page 75)*.

◆ With the vapor barrier facing the finished room, fit batts or blankets between the studs of knee walls *(right)*. Staple the flanges of the insulation to the studs every 6 inches.

◆ From the opening in the flat part of the ceiling, pour loose fill down behind the sloped portion, leaving a 1-inch air space between the insulation and the sheathing. If necessary, push the insulation down with a broom handle.

◆ Cover the area above the flat ceiling with batts or blankets, vapor barrier down; if space is limited, blow in loose fill adapting the technique on page 88, Step 4.

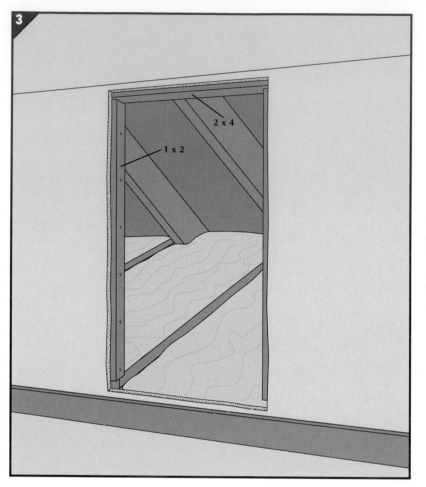

3. Framing the access holes.

◆ With $3\frac{1}{2}$-inch common nails, toenail a 2-by-4 across the top of the opening with its front edge set back $\frac{1}{2}$ inch from the wall surface.

◆ Fasten 1-by-2 strips along the studs or joists on each side of the opening with $2\frac{1}{2}$-inch nails, aligning their front edges with that of the 2-by-4.

4. Adding a removable panel.

◆ Cut a piece of $\frac{1}{2}$-inch plywood to fit the opening. Staple an insulation batt or blanket to the back of the panel, with the vapor barrier facing the room.

◆ Holding the panel in place, screw on as many turn buttons as required to secure it, fastening the buttons to the panel and the framing around the opening *(right)*.

◆ For the ceiling access holes, patch them with wallboard cut to fit.

TURN BUTTON

Getting Insulation Into Exterior Walls

After you have attended to the attic, you can turn next to the exterior walls. The type of insulation you buy and where you install it depends on how the walls are constructed and their condition both inside and out.

Loose Fill or Foam: For a wood-frame house covered with siding, it is usually easiest to blow or pour in loose fill from outside *(pages 86-88)*. To accomplish this you must remove some siding and cut holes in the sheathing to provide access to the spaces between the studs. A special blower can be rented from a building-supply firm or insulation contractor.

By a similar technique you can insulate from inside the house, but the method is more disruptive and difficult to repair. For a masonry wall, however, insulating it from the inside may be the only option.

If you opt for sprayed-in-place foam as an insulating material *(page 89)*, have it installed by a professional. In some cases, you may save money by preparing the walls yourself.

Obstacles in Walls: Whether your house is wood frame or masonry, its wall cavities may contain obstructions. Fire stops—horizontal boards nailed between studs—are especially common in homes built before 1940.

Other obstacles include pipes, heating ducts, and electrical wires. In many cases, it may be necessary to cut access holes in the wall at several places to fill it completely.

Older houses may have continuous spaces between the studs from the attic to the basement. With this type of construction—called balloon-framing—block off the cavities at the basement ceiling and blow in the insulation down from the attic.

Vapor Barriers: When using loose-fill insulation, you must create a vapor barrier by coating the inside walls with a vapor-barrier paint. Foam insulation creates its own barrier.

 TOOLS

Hammer	Pry bar	Hand stapler
Nail set	Utility knife	Electric drill,
Mallet	Mini-hacksaw	extension bit,
Wide-blade	Shingler's	hole saw
putty knife	hatchet	Insulation
Wood chisel	Plumb bob	blower

 **MATERIALS**

1 x 3s	Insulation
Replacement nails	(loose fill, batt,
for siding	rigid board)
Replacement shin-	Insulated backing
gles or shakes	for siding
Common nails ($2\frac{1}{4}$")	Vapor-barrier paint

 **SAFETY TIPS**

Wear safety goggles, a dust mask, and gloves when handling fiberglass.

SHEATHING

Preparing walls for insulation.

First, the top row of siding all around the house is removed. For a two-story house, a strip of siding is also taken off just below the level of the ceiling of the first floor. The location of this strip is identified by drilling a hole with an extension bit through the wall just under the ceiling from inside. Siding immediately below windows and obstructions in the wall such as fire stops are also removed. Such obstructions can be located by performing the test described on page 87, Step 3. A hole is then drilled through the sheathing for each wall cavity between studs.

1. Removing siding.

◆ When the siding is wood shingles or shakes, split the shingle or shake from bottom to top along the grain with a wood chisel and hammer, and pull out the loose pieces.

◆ Pull any protruding nails. For hidden nails, cut them with a mini-hacksaw slipped under the shingles above *(right, top)*.

◆ Cut access holes as shown in Step 3.

◆ For clapboard siding, use a mallet to gently wedge a wide-blade putty knife under the clapboard.

◆ Tap a pry bar between the board and the putty knife *(right, bottom)* and gently pry up the board $\frac{1}{4}$ to $\frac{1}{2}$ inch.

◆ Remove the bar and knife, then tap the board back into place. Pull any protruding nails, then repeat every 16 inches along the board until you have removed all the nails.

◆ Break the paint bond surrounding the board, then pull downward on the board to remove it.

BUILDING PAPER

2. Cutting the access holes.

◆ If there is building paper over the sheathing, cut a flap with a utility knife and peel it down.
◆ Mark holes on the sheathing midway between each pair of studs—nails in the sheathing reveal the stud locations.
◆ With an electric drill fitted with a hole saw large enough to accommodate the nozzle of your blower —which is typically 2 or 3 inches in diameter— cut the holes through the sheathing *(above)*.

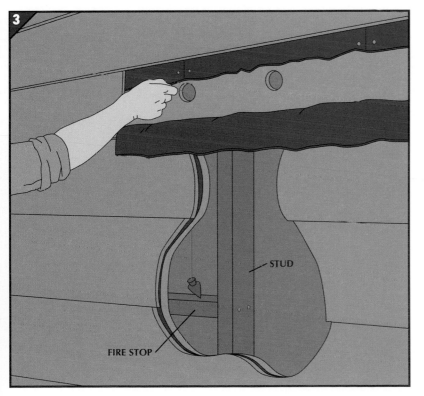

STUD

FIRE STOP

3. Plumbing the wall cavities.

◆ Drop a plumb bob into each access hole to check for braces, fire stops, or other obstructions in the cavities *(left)*.
◆ Drill an access hole below each obstruction in line with the hole you made in Step 3.

4. Blowing in insulation.

◆ Set up the insulation blower following the manufacturer's instructions. Insert the blower nozzle and hose into the hole and down into the cavity.

◆ Gradually fill the cavity with insulation from the bottom up, slowly pulling out the hose as you go *(right)*.

◆ Tip the nozzle up before withdrawing it, filling the space above the hole.

◆ Plug the hole with a sprig of batt insulation.

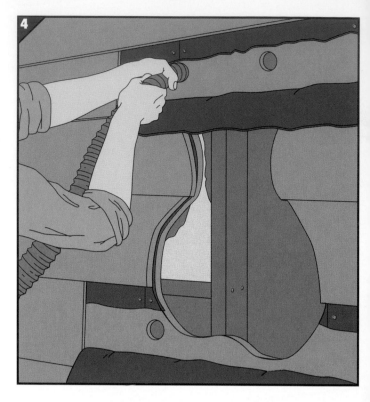

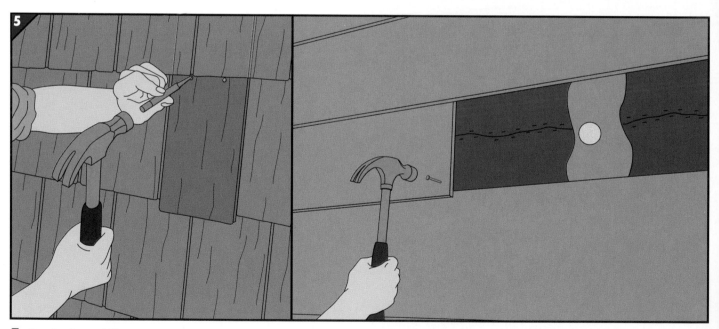

5. Replacing siding.

◆ For shingle or shake siding, use a shingler's hatchet to cut the replacement shingle or shake $\frac{1}{4}$ inch narrower than the gap in the siding.

◆ Slide the piece into position so its bottom extends about $\frac{1}{4}$ inch below the bottom ends of the adjacent pieces.

◆ Drill two pilot holes into the replacement piece along the bottom of the row above. Angle the holes upward.

◆ Drive a nail of the same type and length as those removed into each hole and set the heads with a nail set *(above, left)*.

◆ With a mallet and a wood block, tap the replacement shingle or shake upward so its bottom end is flush with those of the adjacent pieces. Because the nails were driven at an angle, they will straighten out as the shingle or shake is tapped upward.

◆ For clapboard siding, staple the building paper back into position.

◆ Holding the clapboard in position, secure it with nails of the same type and length as those removed *(above, right)*; use the original nail holes in the boards.

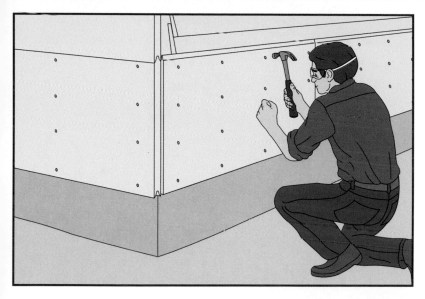

Overlaying rigid foam panels.
Foam insulation panels can be installed over existing siding or sheathing before new siding is applied. Nail 2-by-8-foot insulation panels to the wall with roofing nails long enough to penetrate the sheathing by $\frac{3}{4}$ inch *(left)*. Leave a $\frac{1}{16}$-inch gap at corners to let trapped vapor escape.

Adding insulated backing.
To maximize the insulating properties of new vinyl or aluminum siding, add insulating backing during installation. To do so, nail 1-by-3 furring strips with $2\frac{1}{4}$-inch common nails directly over the existing siding as a base for the new siding. As you position each panel, slip the backing behind it *(right)*.

INSULATING BACKING

SPRAYED-IN-PLACE FOAM INSULATION

Ideal for insulating wall cavities and other inaccessible places, sprayed-in-place foam insulation is simpler to apply than blown-in insulation, but it must be applied by a professional. Because of the small diameter of the applicator nozzle, the foam can be injected through easily patched holes in interior walls *(right)*. All these products, including polyurethane, urea-tripolymer, isocyanurate, and polyicynene, expand to fill all the gaps in a cavity, and they form their own vapor barrier. Polyicynene contains no ozone-depleting CFCs.

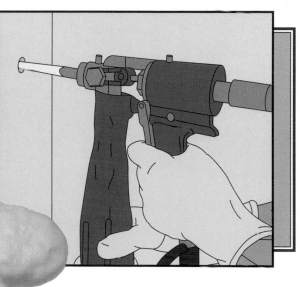

When a basement or crawl space is unheated, unless it is well insulated it may make the floors above it cold, wasting fuel and causing chills. Ducts and pipes passing through the space can also lose heat during cold weather.

Insulating Ceilings and Floors: The first step is to place insulation between the floor joists *(below)*. For a crawl space, or even a basement in an older house, cover dirt floors with plastic sheeting—6-mil or thicker polyethylene *(page 93)*.

Covering Ducts and Pipes: It's best to insulate all exposed heating and air-conditioning ducts in the basement or crawl space. For ducts,

use ready-made duct blankets or standard insulation blankets with a vapor barrier *(opposite)*. Although the vapor barrier normally would be on the side that is warm—against the ducts—in an unheated basement it is more important to protect the insulation from humidity. Therefore, install insulation with the vapor barrier facing out.

Water Pipes: In many cases, insulation around water pipes can prevent them from freezing during winter in cold climates; it also conserves heat in hot water lines during any weather. Buy pipe insulation that fits the diameter of the pipes running through the unheated space.

TOOLS

Utility knife
Hand stapler
Wire brush

MATERIALS

Batt or blanket insulation	Duct tape
	Foam rubber pipe insulation
Insulation supports	Polyethylene sheeting (6-mil)
	2 x 4s or bricks

SAFETY TIPS

Wear safety goggles, a dust mask, gloves, and a long-sleeved shirt when handling fiberglass insulation. Put on a hard hat when working close to joists overhead.

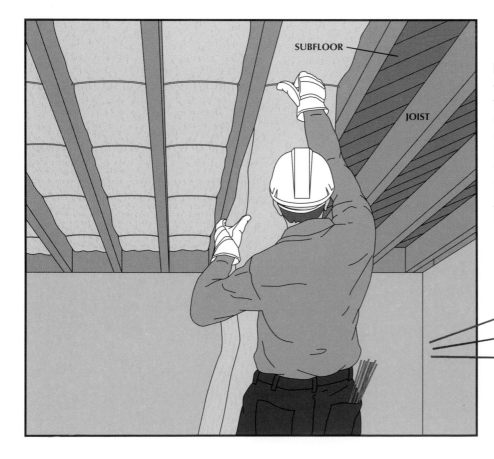

Insulating the ceiling.

◆ Push batt or blanket insulation, with the vapor barrier facing up, into the spaces between the floor joists. Make sure the pieces fit snugly, with the backing lightly touching the subfloor.
◆ Every 16 inches, slide an insulation support *(photograph)* in place between joists, flexing it toward the insulation and exerting slight pressure *(left)*.

WRAPS FOR DUCTS

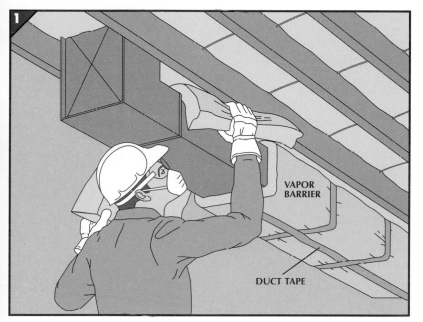

1. Covering the sides of the duct.
◆ Wrap an insulation blanket around the duct, then mark and cut the blanket to length. Use this piece to cut the other sections.
◆ Install the pieces of insulation, sealing the seams along the bottom and between the sections with duct tape.

VAPOR BARRIER

DUCT TAPE

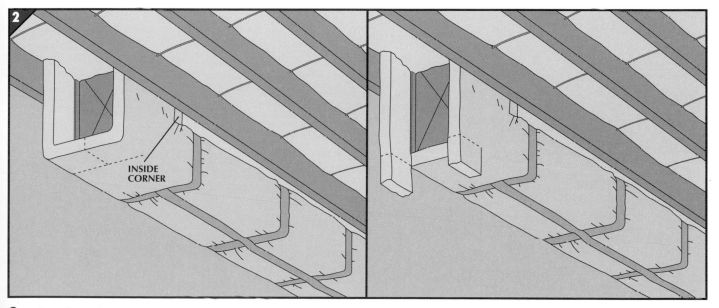

INSIDE CORNER

2. Trimming the end pieces.
◆ Once you've covered most of the horizontal section of duct, cut and apply a narrow piece of insulation to the inside corner where the duct rises to the floor above.
◆ Cut a last section to cover the bottom and sides of the rest of the duct and extend beyond the end by one-half the duct width.
◆ Tape the section to the duct, then make a T-shaped cut in the bottom, as indicated by the dashed lines *(above, left)*, creating two flaps. Cut off the portion of the flaps that extend beyond the bottom of the duct *(above, right)*.

3. Sealing the end of the duct.

◆ Fold the flaps of insulation over the end of the duct, trimming them or adding new material so the ends butt together.

◆ Tape the flaps together securely *(right)*.

◆ If the insulation hangs below head level, cover it with 15-pound building paper to protect it from damage.

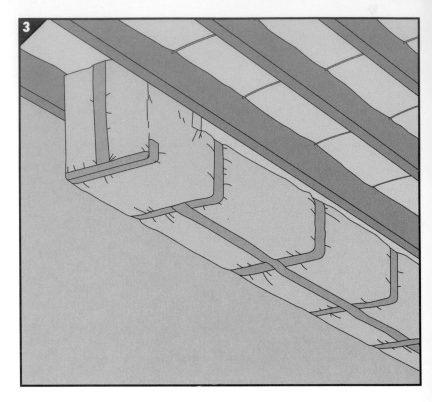

INSULATING A RECESSED DUCT

JOIST

DUCT

Stapling insulation to the joists.

◆ To insulate a duct nestled between joists, cut blanket sections long enough to wrap around the bottom of the duct and cover the edges of the joists.

◆ Push about 1 inch of insulation back from the ends of each section, leaving the vapor barrier intact.

◆ Wrap the insulation around the duct with the vapor barrier facing out, and staple the ends to the joists *(left)*.

◆ Extend the last section of insulation beyond the end of the duct by the thickness of the insulation. Fit a piece of insulation over the end of the duct and seal all the seams with duct tape.

INSTALLING PROTECTIVE PIPE SLEEVES

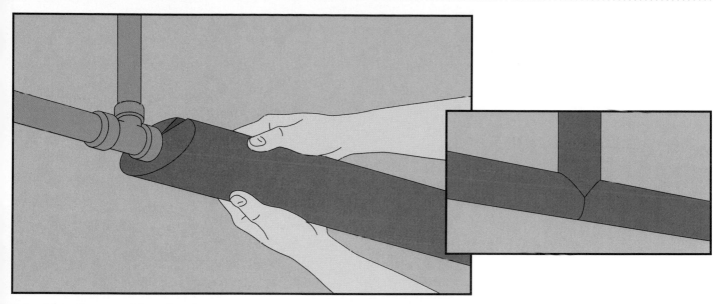

Attaching foam-rubber insulators.
◆ Prepare the pipes by cleaning them, scraping off any rust with a wire brush, and repairing all leaks.
◆ Cut to proper length pieces of foam-rubber pipe insulation that fit the diameter of the pipe.
◆ Open the slit in each tube, and fit the insulation over the pipe *(above)*.

◆ At joints between vertical and horizontal pipe runs, cut a V-shaped wedge at the end of the vertical piece and matching notches in the horizontal ones *(inset)*.

Alternatively, apply self-adhesive aluminum-backed foam insulation tape, wrapping it around the pipe in a continuous, overlapping strip.

A DIRT-FLOOR VAPOR BARRIER

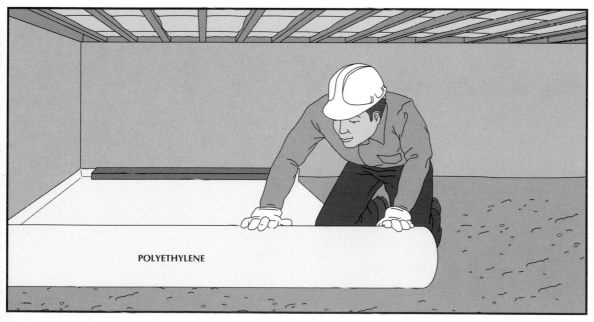

POLYETHYLENE

Laying plastic sheets.
◆ Buy enough 6-mil or thicker polyethylene to cover the floor, allowing for extra material to overlap adjacent sheets by 6 inches.
◆ With the starting end of the roll 2 inches up the wall, hold it in place with 2-by-4s or bricks against the wall, and unroll the sheet across the floor *(above)*.
◆ At the opposite wall, trim the plastic and weigh down the end.
◆ Overlap the edges of subsequent sheets by 6 inches.

Since their functions are dissimilar, heated basements and crawl spaces are not insulated alike. For a basement, it's best to insulate in a way that makes finishing the space easy. A heated crawl space may be used for storage; or, in some houses, it may serve as a huge duct, called a plenum, through which heat passes on its way to the living area above.

Rigid Board for Basements: The extruded polystyrene panels on the following pages are designed to be secured to the walls with nailing strips. Once in place, the panels can easily be covered with gypsum wallboard. In fact, since foam insulation is not fire resistant, most codes require this type of insulation to be covered with $\frac{1}{2}$-inch wallboard.

Accommodating Wiring: When 1-by-3s are used to secure rigid foam insulation, you must cut grooves in the back of panels where electrical

wires pass along the wall, and the wires must be in place before you install the panels. With 2-by-3 nailing strips, there will be a gap between the panels and the wallboard, so the wires can run through this gap. You can position electrical boxes while putting up the insulation and have the wiring done before the wallboard is secured.

Crawl Spaces: Before insulating a heated crawl space that serves as a plenum, consider installing ducts to carry the heated air to the living area—you may save enough money in reduced energy bills to pay for the ductwork. If you don't install ducts, you can greatly reduce heat loss by covering the ground with a polyethylene vapor barrier *(page 93)* and insulating the walls and floor *(page 98)*. The ducts themselves should also be insulated *(page 91)*, or you can simply seal their seams with high-heat duct tape.

TOOLS

Tape measure
Carpenter's
  level
Utility knife
Hand stapler
Circular saw or
  handsaw
Electric drill
Masonry bit
Hammer

MATERIALS

1 x 2s, 1 x 3s
Common nails (3")
Masonry nails
Batt or blanket
  insulation
Rigid-board
  insulation
Insulating
  foam
Polyethylene
  sheeting
Bricks

SAFETY TIPS

Wear goggles when driving nails and when working above eye level.

PUTTING IN RIGID-BOARD INSULATION

1. Insulating the box joists.

◆ On the walls that run parallel to the joists, cut lengths of batt or blanket insulation to cover the joists—called box joists—between the top of the wall and the subfloor.

◆ With the vapor barrier facing into the room, staple the flanges along the edges of the insulation every 6 inches to the subfloor and sole plate *(right)*.

◆ Insulate the headers—the joists that run along the top of the walls perpendicular to the floor joists—with short lengths of insulation.

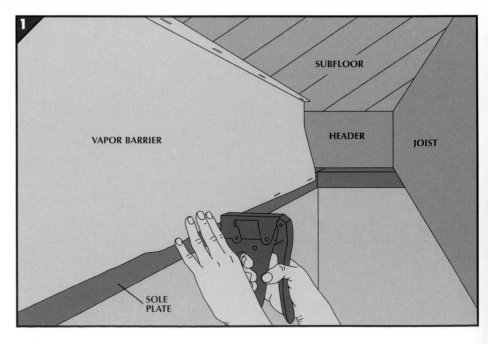

2. Positioning the first panel.

◆ Trim the first panel of rigid-board insulation with a utility knife to fit between the basement floor and the joists. It isn't necessary to cut through the panel completely—simply cut halfway through, align the cut with the edge of a table, and snap the waste piece off.

◆ Starting in the middle of one wall, hold and plumb the panel against the wall *(left)*, then have a helper hold it in position.

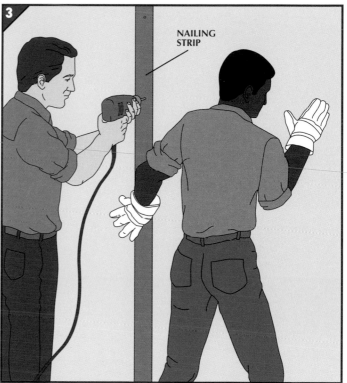

NAILING STRIP

3. Preparing the nailing strips.

◆ Position a second panel next to the first and fit a 1-by-3 or a 2-by-3 nailing strip in the groove between the panels.

◆ With your helper holding both panels in position, drill clearance holes through the strip that are slightly smaller than the diameter of the nails you will be driving. Position holes 4 inches from the top and bottom, and one in the middle. If the wall will be holding shelves, drill two more holes, centering them between the others *(right)*.

TRICKS OF THE TRADE

Mark and Measure in One Step

A tape measure can double as a pencil and straightedge for marking rigid insulation panels. Lock the tape at the desired length and, holding the body against the end of the panel, pull the tape across it. The hook will etch a cutting mark into the panel.

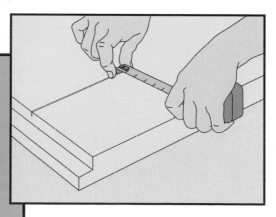

4. Nailing the panels to the wall.

Drive masonry nails $1\frac{1}{4}$ inches longer than the thickness of the panels into each hole in the nailing strips and panels, and into the wall *(right)*.

Alternatively, use masonry screws—drive them with an electric drill fitted with a screwdriver bit.

5. Securing the corners.

At inside corners *(far left)*, first trim a panel to width and butt the trimmed edge against one side of the corner. Then position a second panel against the first—cutting any excess width from its middle to preserve both grooved edges. Secure the panels with a 1-by-2 or 2-by-2 nailing strip and fasteners as described in Steps 3 and 4.

At outside corners *(near left)*, use masonry nails to secure a strip the same thickness as the insulation to the wall flush with the corner; then, with common nails, fasten another strip to the first one in line with the adjoining wall. Position insulation along the walls, butting the first panels against the strips.

NAILING STRIP

MASONRY NAIL

COMMON NAIL

FITTING PANELS AROUND OBSTACLES

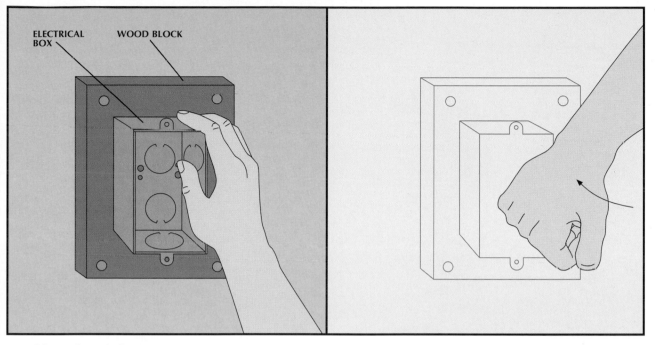

ELECTRICAL BOX

WOOD BLOCK

Marking electric boxes.

◆ When panels are thicker than the depth of a standard electrical box, mount the box on a wood block and fasten the block to the wall with masonry nails as shown *(above, left)* so the front of the box will extend past the panel by the thickness of the wallboard.

◆ Hold the panel in its correct position on the wall and tap it sharply to mark the placement of the box *(above, right)*.

◆ Cut out the opening for the box with a utility knife.

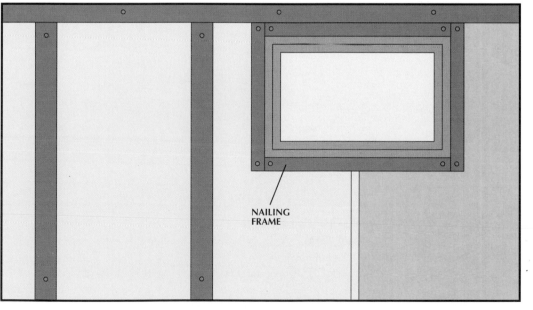

NAILING FRAME

Framing openings and obstacles.

◆ Cut nailing strips to frame windows and doors.

◆ Fasten the strips around the windows and doors with their inside edges flush with the outside of the framing.

◆ Cut insulation panels to fit flush against the strips, as shown above.

◆ Secure the grooved edges of the panels with nailing strips and fasteners.

To insulate around pipes and ducts, frame them as closely as possible and install insulation around them as you would around windows. Then fill in the spaces around the objects with a compatible insulating foam.

1. Insulating the box-joist walls.

◆ Lay a single strip of polyethylene vapor barrier *(page 93)* along the ground next to the box-joist walls—the walls that run parallel to the joists.

◆ Cut lengths of batt or blanket insulation to fit between the ground and the subfloor above.

◆ With the vapor barrier facing into the room, position the insulation against the wall, securing the top end with a 1-by-2 fastened with 3-inch common nails to the box joist along the top of the wall *(left)*. Butt the edges of successive blanket lengths together tightly and secure them in place.

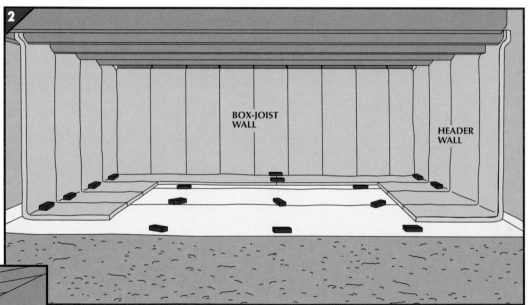

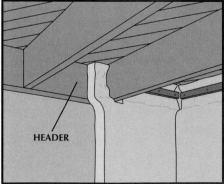

2. Insulating the header walls and floor.

◆ For the header walls—those perpendicular to the joists—position a batt or blanket at the end farthest from the exit, butting it tightly against the first piece on the box-joist wall.

◆ Notch the blanket to fit around the joist, then secure it to the header with a 1-by-2 cut to fit between the joists *(inset)*.

◆ Run the blanket down the wall to the middle of the floor, then fasten a matching piece on the opposite wall. Weigh down the insulation at the base of the walls and at the point where the two lengths meet with bricks or 2-by-4s.

◆ Fill gaps in the corners with scrap pieces of insulation.

◆ Lay a second strip of vapor barrier on the ground and fasten a second length of insulation to each header wall, cutting the lengths to cover 2 feet of floor.

◆ Weigh the insulation and sheeting down.

◆ Continue laying sheeting and insulation *(above)*. For the last section, finish the wall with two lengths of insulation that meet in the middle of the floor.

INSULATING AND WEATHERPROOFING

BY THE EDITORS OF TIME-LIFE BOOKS, ALEXANDRIA, VIRGINIA

The Consultants

Tim Grether, the Technical Service Manager for Insulation North America at Owens Corning, concentrates on energy conservation and the correct installation of insulation products. The editor of *The Energy Insider*, he also contributes to other trade publications, and is a spokesperson for the North American Insulation Manufacturers Association.

Jeff Palumbo is a registered journeyman carpenter who has a home-building and remodeling business in northern Virginia. His interest in carpentry was sparked by his grandfather, a master carpenter with more than 50 years' experience. Mr. Palumbo teaches in the Fairfax County Adult Education Program.

Mark M. Steele is a professional home inspector in the Washington, D.C., area. He has developed and conducted training programs in home-ownership skills for first-time homeowners. He appears frequently on television and radio as an expert in home repair and consumer topics.

An Array of Storm Windows

During cold weather, a house can lose up to 25 percent of its heat through its windows. The weather-stripping techniques in Chapter 1 can mitigate this loss, but they cannot compensate for the fact that glass is a poor insulator. Adding a storm window can double the insulating capacity of the window *(below and pages 100-102)*. Another option is to replace the sashes *(page 15)*, or to replace windows and frames with energy-efficient units.

Preserving Historic Windows: The beauty of original windows can often be ruined by exterior storm windows, so much so that they are even banned in some historic areas. In such situations, storm windows—custom made to match the size and style of the windows—can be installed on the inside *(page 102)*.

 TOOLS

Tape measure
Hammer
Screwdriver
Electric drill
High-speed
  steel bit
Caulking gun

 **MATERIALS**

Galvanized sheet-metal
  screws ($\frac{3}{4}$" No. 8)
Galvanized wood
  screws ($\frac{3}{4}$" No. 8)
Screw eyes and hooks
Vent plugs
Caulk

 **SAFETY TIPS**

Wear safety goggles when using power tools or hammering.

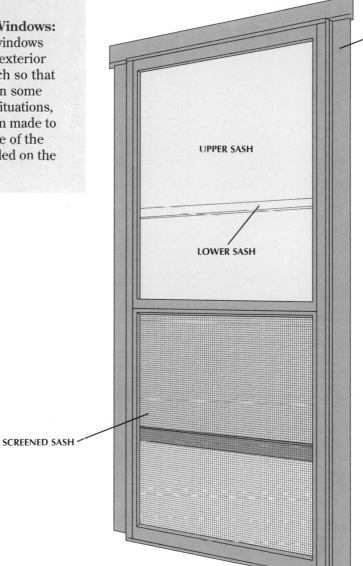

FLANGE

UPPER SASH

LOWER SASH

SCREENED SASH

Anatomy of a storm window.

Exterior storm windows like the one shown at left can be ordered with built-in weather stripping and a flange that matches the brickmold of the existing window. The flange is designed to be nailed to the brickmold. If the window has no weather stripping, seal the gap between the flange and the existing window with foam-rubber tape *(pages 8-9)*.

This type of combination storm window is permanently installed, and provides you with a screened lower sash for the warmer season.

MOUNTING A SIMPLE BARRIER AGAINST THE WEATHER

1. Measuring the opening.
Window frames are often slightly asymmetrical or out of square. To determine the size of storm window you need, measure the height of the opening between the head jamb and sill at both sides and its width between the brickmolds at the top, middle, and bottom. Use the lesser of each measurement when ordering the window.

2. Hanging the window.
Both aluminum and wood storm windows of the type shown above pivot from two brackets at the top, and are held tight against the window with a hook and eye. Usually the brackets are packaged with the window.
◆ With $\frac{3}{4}$-inch sheet-metal screws, attach the bottom leaf of each bracket to the upper rail of the storm window, positioning them 3 inches from the corner.
◆ Hold the storm window in place against the win-

dow and mark the screw holes in the top half of each bracket on the top jamb.
◆ Drill a hole at each mark and screw the top brackets in place.
◆ Hook the window in the top brackets, then align it as necessary by adjusting the screws in their elongated slots in the bottom brackets *(inset)*.
◆ Finally attach a hook to the lower rail and a matching screw eye to the sill.

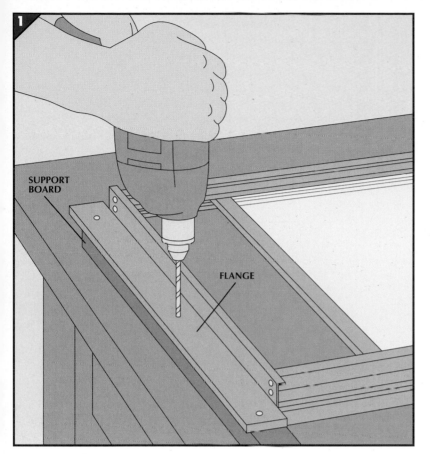

1. Preparing the window.

Unless the window comes with predrilled screw holes, you will need to drill them.

◆ Set the window on a flat work surface and support one of the flanges with a support board.

◆ With a high-speed steel bit, drill three $\frac{3}{16}$-inch clearance holes through the flange—one $\frac{3}{4}$ inch from each end and one in the middle *(left)*. Repeat with the other flanges.

◆ If there is no weather stripping on the flanges, apply a bead of caulk along their inside surfaces.

2. Fastening the window.

◆ With a helper inside holding the storm window in position, drive a $\frac{3}{4}$-inch No. 8 galvanized wood screw through the middle hole on one side flange *(right)*.

◆ Center the window against the frame and drive the middle screw on the opposite side. Drive the remaining screws.

STORM WINDOWS THAT FIT INSIDE

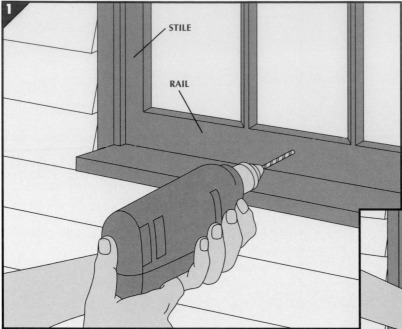

STILE

RAIL

1. Drilling vent holes.

◆ Determine the size of window needed as for an exterior storm window (page 100), but work inside to measure between the rails and stiles.

◆ To prevent condensation from forming between the existing window and the interior storm window, work outside to drill a $\frac{1}{4}$-inch hole 1 inch deep into the middle of the lower rail (left).

◆ Inside, drill a hole into the top of the rail that intersects with the first hole.

◆ Tap a vent plug—often supplied with the window—into each hole (inset).

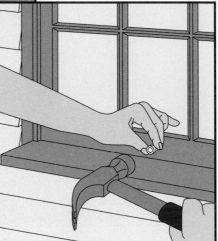

2. Fastening the window.

◆ For each turn button supplied with the window—they're typically spaced 18 inches apart—drill a $\frac{1}{16}$-inch pilot hole into the window sash $\frac{1}{4}$ inch from the stop.

◆ Screw the turn buttons to the rails, leaving the screws a little loose.

◆ Position the storm window, swivel the turn buttons to secure it in place, and finish tightening the buttons (right).

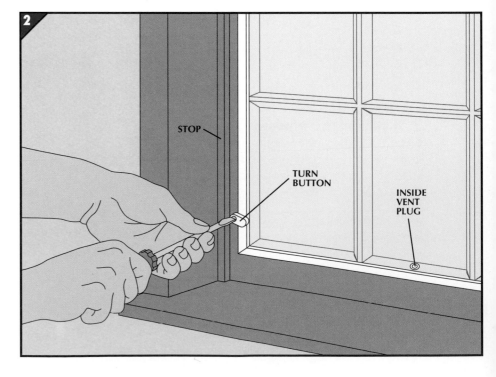

STOP

TURN BUTTON

INSIDE VENT PLUG

Exterior doors can be a source of heat loss whenever they are opened. One remedy is to build a mud room or foyer to serve as an air lock. A more modest proposition is to add a storm door to the main exterior door *(page 104)*. It's best to position the hinges on the same side as those of the existing door so the two doors needn't be opened wide when they are passed through.

Installation: Although putting a storm door in place isn't as demanding a job as hanging an exterior door, it's best to have a helper on hand to hold the door in position while you fasten it to the existing jamb. Like any door, a storm door should be plumb, so you may need to insert wood shims between the door's frame and the jambs.

Once the storm door is in place, the strike plate must be fastened to the jamb. Most models include metal shims for the plate to ensure that it interlocks with the latch bolt.

Weather Stripping: The space between the door and frame is typically sealed with built-in weather stripping. If there is no weather stripping between the storm door's frame and the door jambs, apply one or two beads of caulk on the frame just before securing it.

 TOOLS

Tape measure	Hacksaw
Carpenter's level	File
Screwdriver	Electric drill

 **MATERIALS**

Galvanized common nail (2")	Galvanized sheet metal screws ($\frac{1}{2}$" No. 10)
Galvanized wood screws ($\frac{3}{4}$" No. 8, 1" No. 12)	Shims

 **SAFETY TIPS**

Wear goggles when using a drill.

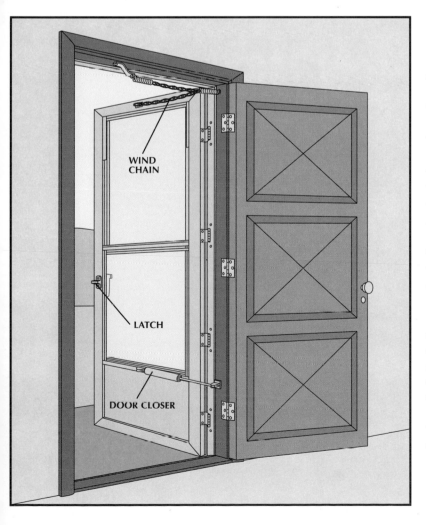

WIND CHAIN

LATCH

DOOR CLOSER

Anatomy of a storm door.
Storm doors are usually available with all the elements shown at left. The wind chain, for example, prevents the door from swinging open abruptly if it is caught by the wind. The frame is custom-made to fit the existing door jambs and is secured to them; hardware and fasteners are included. Often, the sides are left a bit long and are trimmed to fit *(page 104, Step 1)*. Shims—thin pieces of wood driven between the frame and jambs—are used to plumb the door and compensate for any gaps once it is installed *(page 104, Step 2)*.

Both right- and left-hinged storm doors are available. On most models, the window can be replaced with a screen for summer. An alternative is a combination door, which features a double-hung window with a screen on the lower half. Unlike the screen on a standard door, the window on a combination type can be closed when it rains.

PUTTING IN THE DOOR

1. Preparing the frame.

To determine the size storm door needed, take three measurements for the width of the door—at the top, middle, and bottom. Measure the height at each side and in the middle. Record the lesser of the two sets of measurements.

Follow the manufacturer's instructions for preparing your storm door. For the model shown, use a hacksaw to cut the sides of the frame to the recorded height measurement less $\frac{1}{4}$ inch. Remove any sharp burrs with a file.

2. Hanging the door.

◆ Set the door-and-frame assembly in place with the back butted against the doorstop.
◆ Open the door and have a helper support it in position.
◆ With a carpenter's level, check the door for plumb, and drive shims between its frame and the jambs, if necessary.
◆ Secure the storm door frame to the jambs with $\frac{3}{4}$-inch No. 8 galvanized wood screws.

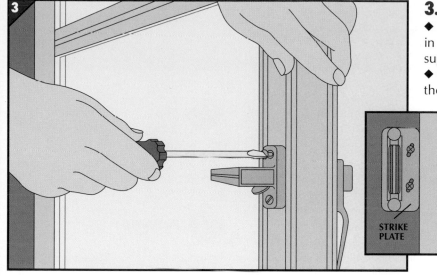

3. Fitting the latch and handle.

◆ Fit the handle and latch into their openings in the door and attach them with the screws supplied *(left)*.

◆ Close the door, mark the latch location on the jamb, position the strike plate, and mark its screw holes.

◆ Drill a pilot hole into the jamb at each mark and screw the strike plate in place *(inset)*. Close the door and check the strike plate position. If the latch bolt and strike plate don't engage properly, unscrew the plate, and slip one or more of the metal shims provided between it and the jamb before refastening.

STRIKE PLATE

4. Attaching the door closer.

◆ Position the jamb bracket on the hinge jamb, close to the handle but below the glass, $\frac{1}{4}$ inch inside the door. Mark the screw holes, drill a $\frac{1}{8}$-inch pilot hole at each mark, and fasten the bracket to the jamb with 1-inch No. 12 wood screws.

◆ Attach the closer rod to the jamb bracket with the pin provided. Hold the door bracket against the door and mark its screw holes.

◆ Remove the closer and offset each door-bracket mark $\frac{1}{4}$ inch toward the side of the door with the handle. Drill a pilot hole at each new mark.

◆ Replace the closer and fasten the door bracket with $\frac{1}{2}$-inch No. 10 sheet-metal screws *(right)*.

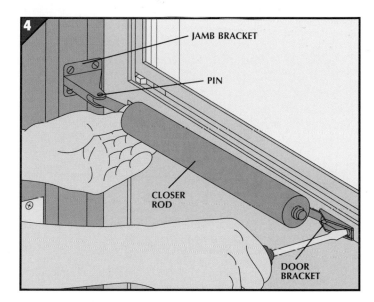

JAMB BRACKET

PIN

CLOSER ROD

DOOR BRACKET

5. Mounting the wind chain.

◆ Secure the wind chain's jamb bracket to the middle of the head jamb with 1-inch No. 12 wood screws.

◆ With the door closed, center the door bracket on the upper rail of the door and mark its screw holes.

◆ Drill a pilot hole at each mark and fasten the door bracket in place with $\frac{1}{2}$-inch No. 10 sheet metal screws *(left)*.

◆ Adjust the length of the chain so the door opens no wider than the closer permits.

◆ Attach the spring to the side jamb with a galvanized 2-inch common nail, then hook the spring to the middle link of the chain.

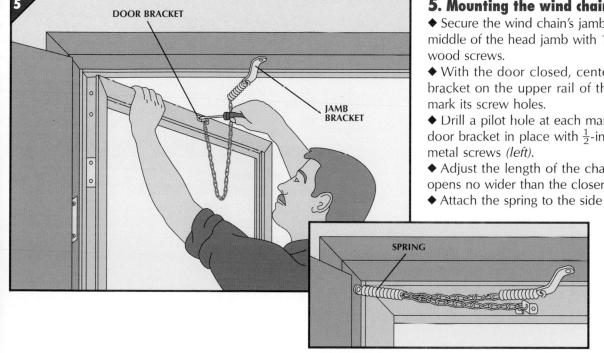

DOOR BRACKET

JAMB BRACKET

SPRING

Blocking Out the Sun

The most important step you can take to ease the burden on your home's air-conditioning system is reducing the amount of sunlight entering the house. Awnings are an excellent way to deflect unwanted sunshine. On their own, they can lower interior temperatures by as much as 8° to 15°. But they needn't transform a house into a dingy dungeon; retractable types let the sun in on cooler days.

A Choice of Material: The traditional material, canvas, is the most inexpensive. But modern synthetics, like nylon, acrylic, and polyester, perform better and last longer. Your supplier can help you choose the best material for your budget.

Installing Awnings: Available in kits, awnings typically come with all the necessary hardware. Mounting details vary depending on the size, style, and brand; one popular style is illustrated here.

Plastic Window Shields: Another way to beat the heat is with plastic window films. Held in place by electrostatic pressure or a self-adhesive backing, these shields deflect heat so well that, in some cases, air-conditioning needs are cut by half.

TOOLS

Tape measure
Chalk line
Carpenter's level

Screwdriver
Socket wrench
Electric drill
Squeegee
Razor blade

MATERIALS

Awning kit
Window film
Galvanized wood
  screws (2" No. 8)

Lag screws
($\frac{5}{16}$" x $1\frac{1}{4}$"),
washers
Shims

SAFETY TIPS

Wear goggles when using power tools.

MEASURING FOR AWNINGS

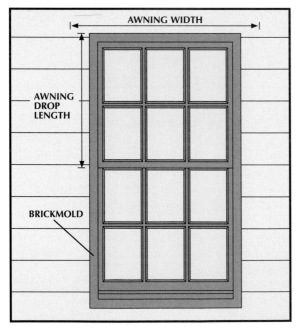

AWNING WIDTH

AWNING DROP LENGTH

BRICKMOLD

Double-hung windows.
◆ Determine the length of the awning drop by measuring from the top of the window brickmold to the middle of the window, as shown above.
◆ Establish the width of the awning by measuring from jamb to jamb at the inside of the brickmolds, and adding 8 inches.

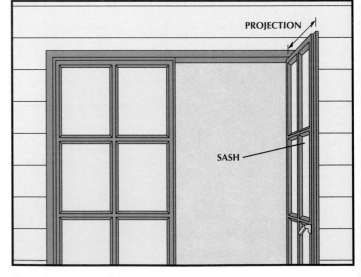

PROJECTION

SASH

Casement windows.
◆ Determine the length of the awning drop and the awning width as for a double-hung window.
◆ Measure the projection of the sash—the distance from the exterior wall to the outer edge of the window sash when it is fully opened. The awning will have to be hung higher to clear this projection.

INSTALLING A ROLL-UP AWNING

SHIM

MOUNTING BRACKET

UPPER-SASH RAIL

1. Attaching the mounting brackets.
◆ On the wall above the window, snap a level chalk line for the top edge of the awning hood so its roller tube will sit slightly above the window's upper-sash rail.
◆ With 2-inch galvanized No. 8 wood screws, attach the mounting brackets $\frac{1}{4}$ inch below the chalk line *(left)*; position them 6 inches from each end of the hood when it is put in place *(below)*.
◆ If the brackets sit unevenly on the siding and brickmold, place shims under them so they rest flat.

2. Hanging the hood.
◆ Hook the hood over the brackets *(right)*, sliding it sideways as necessary so it is centered over the window.
◆ With a socket wrench, tighten the sliding track bolts on the lower edge of the hood.

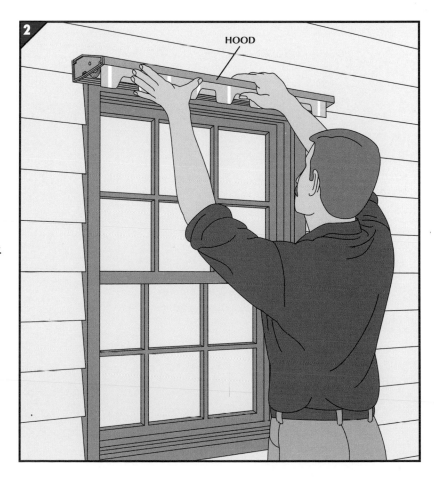

HOOD

3. Attaching the arm.
◆ Measure the projection of the awning less $1\frac{1}{4}$ inches—this will be the distance between the bottom of the hood and the top edge of the arm bracket.
◆ Hold the arm with the bracket in position and mark the screw holes.
◆ Drill a pilot hole at each mark, then secure the bracket with $1\frac{1}{4}$-inch long $\frac{5}{16}$-inch lag screws *(left)*.
◆ Fasten the other arm the same way.

ARM BRACKET

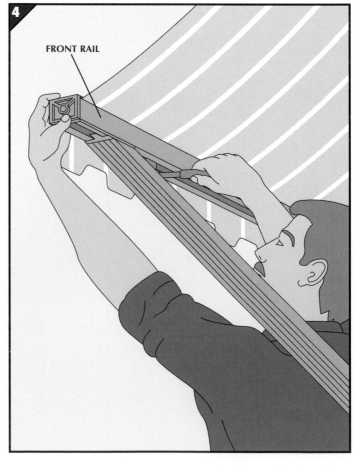

FRONT RAIL

4. Attaching the front rail.
◆ Fully extend the awning; then, slide the bolt at the end of each arm into its groove in the front rail. Tighten the bolts with a socket wrench *(right)*.
◆ Adjust the arms as necessary until they are both at 90 degrees to the wall in the horizontal plane. If the awning is slightly askew, adjust the arms in very small increments until the awning is level.

APPLYING WINDOW FILM

1. Preparing the window.
◆ Wash the inside of the window, scraping off grit with a razor blade.
◆ Cut pieces of plastic film slightly larger than each pane.
◆ Mist the glass with water, peel the protective liner from the film, and mist the side of the film that will bond to the window.
◆ Apply the film to the glass, mist it, and lightly pass over the surface with a squeegee *(left)*.

2. Trimming the film.
◆ Trim the film along the edges of the sash with a razor blade *(right)*.
◆ Mist the film again and pass the squeegee from the top down to remove as much water as possible from beneath the film. Finish by drying the edges of the glass with a lint-free cloth.

The window will be hazy until all moisture trapped behind the film evaporates—a process that may last more than a week.

Protecting Your Home From Disaster

Few areas of the country are immune to natural disaster. Violent winds, earthquakes, lightning strikes, and flooding are all part of the landscape. You can put up a good defense against the elements by safeguarding windows from wind, anchoring masonry chimneys, and grounding TV antennas. In the event of a flood, it's possible to clean up in a way that minimizes damage.

Building a window cover →

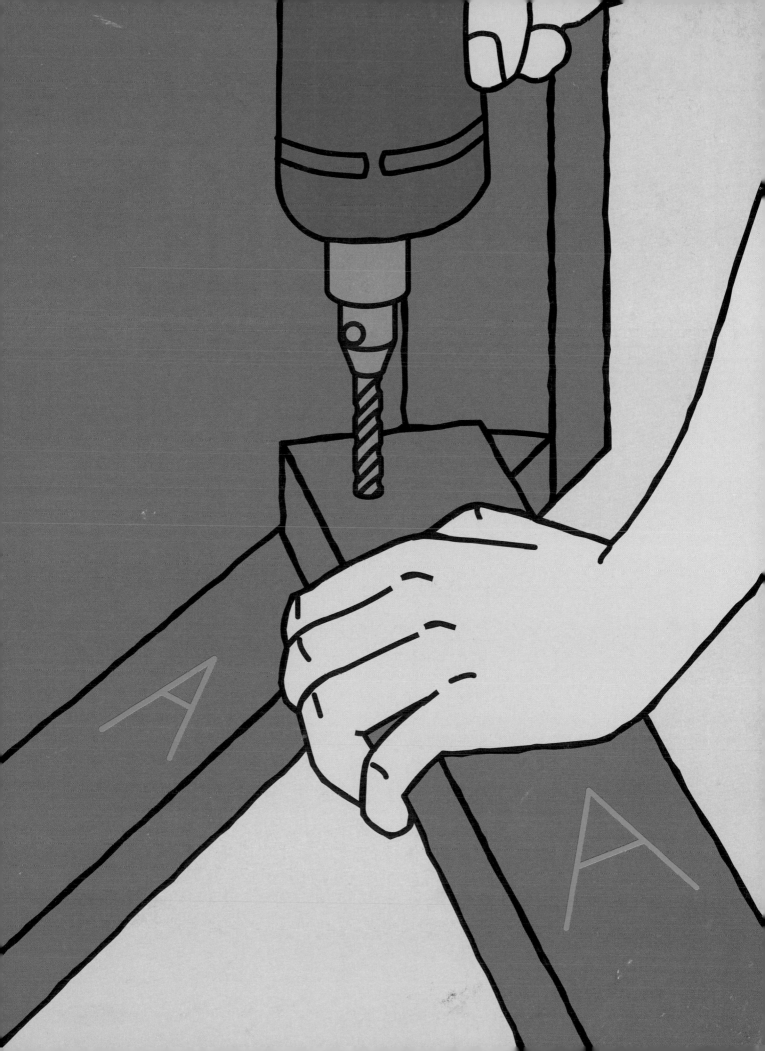

Pushing with immense pressure and tossing objects around like missiles, powerful winds—100 miles per hour and stronger—can easily shatter window glass. If you live in an area subject to violent winds, such as the Atlantic and Gulf coasts, you must be ready to cover your windows quickly when such winds are forecast.

Plywood Shields: Shutters are an adequate windbreak, but picture windows usually are too large to shutter—and simply nailing boards across them may damage the frame or siding. For ground-floor picture windows, which are the most common sort, the $\frac{1}{2}$-inch plywood cover illustrated on these pages offers complete protection. Designed as a knockdown assembly, you can build the cover at any time and store it,

ready to be deployed when needed. Fitting between the sill and the drip cap outside the casing, it does not scratch the glass. Angled 2-by-4s, anchored to the ground by stakes, hold the cover firmly.

Blocking for Smaller Windows: For standard windows without shutters, $\frac{1}{2}$-inch plywood covers can be cut to fit over the panes and brickmold, or exterior casing. Drill holes in the wood $\frac{3}{4}$ inch from the edges at 18-inch intervals and secure the covers to the brickmold with $2\frac{1}{2}$-inch common nails. Label each cover so you know where it goes.

Tidying Up: Don't give strong winds anything to buffet—trim dead or weak branches on your property, and tie down lightweight objects or bring them inside.

TOOLS

Tape measure
Hammer

Maul
Handsaw
Circular saw
Electric drill

MATERIALS

2 x 4s
$\frac{1}{2}$" exterior-grade plywood
Double-headed nails (3")

Galvanized common nails (2", $2\frac{1}{2}$", $3\frac{1}{2}$")
Carriage bolts ($\frac{3}{8}$" x 4")
Wood battens

SAFETY TIPS

Wear goggles when driving nails or operating a power tool.

BUILDING A WINDOW COVER

1. Sizing the cover and supports.
◆ For the cover's height, measure the height of the window from the bottom of the drip cap to the top of the sill. For the width, measure between the outside edges of side brickmolds.
◆ Cut a piece of $\frac{1}{2}$-inch exterior-grade plywood to the measurements. If necessary, join two panels together, reinforcing the seam with wood battens.
◆ For the supports to be installed in Step 3, measure from the bottom of the drip cap to the ground and multiply this figure by 1.5; then, cut the two supports to that length.

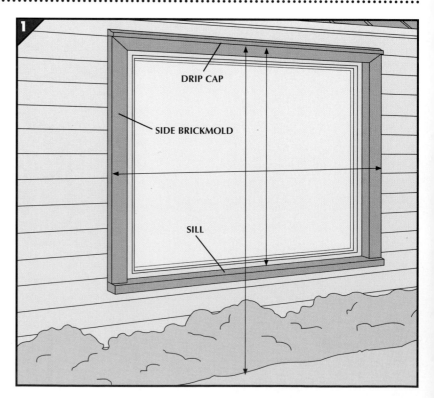

DRIP CAP

SIDE BRICKMOLD

SILL

2. Assembling the cover.

◆ Cut four 2-by-4s to frame the plywood.
◆ Set the plywood down flat, position the 2-by-4s on edge around the sides, and fasten the boards together with $3\frac{1}{2}$-inch galvanized common nails *(above)*.
◆ Turn the assembly over and fasten the plywood to the frame with 2-inch nails at 6- to 8-inch intervals.

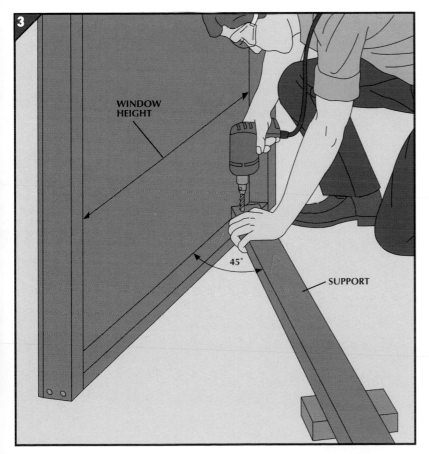

WINDOW HEIGHT

45°

SUPPORT

3. Preparing the supports.

◆ Stand the cover on its side and place one support in the upper corner of the frame at a 45-degree angle. Hold the support level with a scrap 2-by-4.
◆ Drill a $\frac{3}{8}$-inch hole through the support and frame *(left)*. Label both pieces at the corner with a reference letter so you can assemble the cover quickly.
◆ Turn the cover over and prepare the other support the same way.

4. Deploying the cover.

◆ Stand the cover on the ground in front of the window with the frame facing the glass.

◆ Attach the supports to the frame with $\frac{3}{8}$-by-4-inch carriage bolts.

◆ Position the cover on the window sill *(right)*. If necessary, loosen the bolts and adjust the angle of the supports so they rest on the ground and hold the cover against the window.

5. Bracing the supports.

◆ Measure from the bottom corner of the frame straight out to the outside edge of one support.

◆ Cut two 2-by-4 braces to your measurement and fasten them to the frame and inside face of the supports with 3-inch double-headed nails *(above)*.

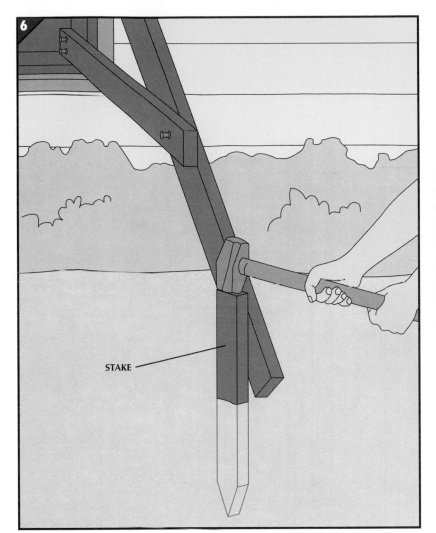

6. Anchoring the cover.

◆ Cut two 2-by-4s 2 feet long and trim an end of each one to a point, forming stakes.

◆ With a maul, drive a stake into the ground beside the bottom of each support *(left)*. Fasten the stakes to the supports with 3-inch double-headed nails.

◆ To store the cover until you need it, remove the braces, supports, and stakes. Keep the pieces in a handy location.

STAKE

PERMANENT STORM SHUTTERS

Storm shutters provide window protection that is more elegant and convenient than plywood covers. Also known as Florida shutters and hurricane shutters, they are designed to mount permanently to the exterior of the house. Usually made of aluminum, they look like wood shutters, but they offer significantly more protection against flying debris.

Among the many types of storm shutters available, the model shown is the simplest to install and operate. Hinged at the top, it can be raised to screen out the sun. In windy conditions, the shutter is lowered and latched tight against the house. Another type is mounted vertically on each side of the window and slides across the panes when danger looms. Accordion shutters can be drawn across the window by hand. Even more substantial are roll-out shutters that close by means of a rack and pinion drive system operated from inside the house. You can even buy systems that automatically monitor the sun and wind, and adjust the shutters accordingly with motorized controls.

Chimney Ties for Earth Tremors

While a solidly built wood-frame house stands an excellent chance of surviving an earthquake, one with an exterior masonry chimney does not. When the ground starts shaking, the house and chimney respond as separate structures, pounding against each other or pulling apart.

Metal Strapping: In areas subject to earthquakes, masonry chimneys on most new homes are steel-reinforced and attached to the frame with steel ties. On older homes, chimneys can be safeguarded with exterior metal straps secured to the house, as shown below. Cutting and shaping these straps is fairly straightforward *(page 118)*, but they can also be custom-made by a metal supplier.

On a two-story house, the chimney is anchored at two points. You can conceal the portion of the lower strap that runs along the wall by removing some of the siding, securing the strap to the sheathing, and refastening the siding. A single strap in the attic is adequate to anchor a chimney to a one-story house.

When working at heights, use ladders safely *(page 28)*.

Earthquake Protection: Additional steps you can take to quake-proof your home depend on where you live. Measures typically involve using bolts or metal ties to bolster the bond between the frame and the foundation and between floors. Compare your home's status to code requirements for new construction in your area and consult a professional if you wish to correct any deficencies.

 TOOLS

Tape measure	Keyhole saw
Carpenter's level	Circular saw
Hammer	Clamps
Wrench	Electric drill
Hacksaw	High-speed steel bit
	Propane torch
	Caulking gun

 **MATERIALS**

2 x 4s	Lag screws
Plywood	($\frac{3}{8}$" x $1\frac{1}{2}$", 3")
Common nails	and washers
($3\frac{1}{2}$", 6")	Steel strapping
	($\frac{3}{16}$" x $1\frac{1}{4}$")
	Exterior caulk

 **SAFETY TIPS**

Wear goggles when driving nails; put on a hard hat when working in an unfinished attic. Don goggles and work gloves when operating a propane torch.

A chimney tied to a house.
In a two-story house, two metal straps are wrapped around the chimney. One is secured to the exterior wall and header joist between the first and second floors. The other passes through the wall and is attached to 2-by-4 braces laid diagonally across three ceiling joists in the attic. In a finished attic, the floor must be raised to cover the second strap.

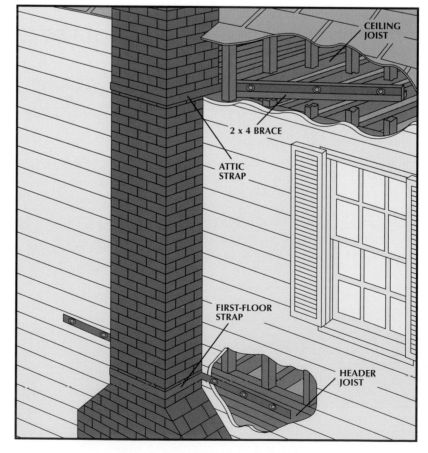

1. Marking for the lower strap.

◆ From inside, mark the first-floor header joist by measuring from the top casing of a window near the chimney to the ceiling and adding $2\frac{1}{2}$ inches; transfer the measurement to the exterior wall. If there is no nearby window, drive a 6-inch nail through the wall near the chimney at ceiling height and mark the outside wall $2\frac{1}{2}$ inches above the nail. Remove the nail and patch the wall.

◆ At the mark, draw a level line along the wall and across the chimney; then extend it 3 feet on each side of the chimney (left).

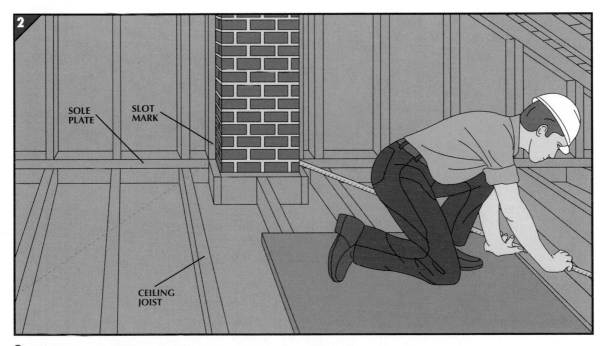

SOLE PLATE

SLOT MARK

CEILING JOIST

2. Marking for the attic strap.

◆ When the chimney is exposed in the attic, mark locations for the wall slots on the studs at each side of the chimney $1\frac{3}{4}$ inches above the sole plate. If the chimney is not exposed in the attic, locate the studs adjacent to it from outside: Drive a nail through the wall on each side of the chimney high enough to clear the top plate.

◆ To determine the strap length, extend a measuring tape at a 45-degree angle from one slot mark toward the opposite wall across three ceiling joists (above). Double this length and add the measurement of the outside perimeter of the chimney plus 1 foot.

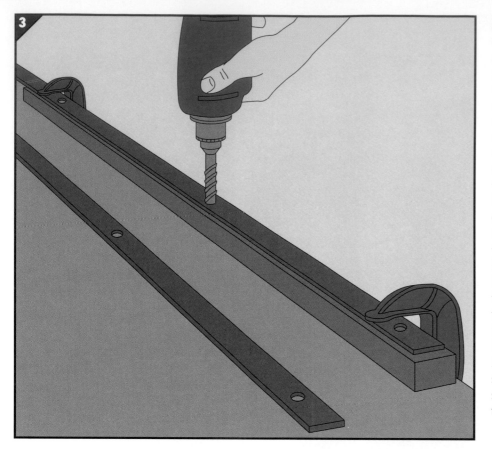

3. Preparing the straps.

◆ With a hacksaw, cut $\frac{3}{16}$-by-1$\frac{1}{4}$-inch strap iron or steel to the lengths you measured in Steps 1 and 2.

◆ To mark the bends on the lower chimney strap, scribe a line across the strap 3 feet from each end; add another pair of lines inside the first set offset by the length of the sides of the chimney less $\frac{1}{4}$ inch.

◆ For the attic strap, mark a pair of lines at a distance from each end equal to the diagonal measurement made in Step 2.

◆ With the strap clamped to a backup board, mark holes for the lower strap 2 inches from each end, then 2 inches from the outermost scribed lines, and finally midway between the first set of holes. For the attic strap, mark the two innermost holes so they will lie at least 2 inches from the chimney when the strap is in place. With a high-speed steel bit, drill a $\frac{1}{2}$-inch hole through the straps at each mark *(left)*.

4. Shaping the straps.

◆ Clamp the lower strap in a metal vise with one of the inside bend marks just outside the jaws.

◆ Play the flame from a propane torch across the strap at the vise until the strap glows red across its width; then, bend the end out to form a 90-degree angle. Repeat for the other inside bend and the two outside bends *(right)*.

◆ For the attic strap, bend the metal 90 degrees at each bend mark, shaping the strap into a U.

◆ Dip the hot metal in water to cool it before handling it without gloves.

⚠️ **CAUTION** *When operating a propane torch, remove all flammable objects from the area and keep a fire extinguisher handy.*

5. Bolting the lower strap.

◆ Working with a helper, position the strap on the wall and chimney. With the bottom aligned with the level line on the wall, mark the bolt holes, then take the strap down.

◆ Drill a $\frac{1}{4}$-inch-diameter hole into the wall and header joist at each mark.

◆ Secure the strap to the wall with $\frac{3}{8}$-by-3-inch lag screws and washers, tightening the bolts with a wrench (left).

6. Placing the attic strap.

◆ Inside the attic, drill $\frac{1}{4}$-inch holes through the stud and wall at the slot marks. With a keyhole saw, finish cutting the slots to accommodate the straps.

◆ With a helper, slide the ends of the strap into the slots (right). Push the strap tight against the chimney.

7. Bracing the attic strap.

◆ Cut four 2-by-4 braces to fit between the chimney and the ends of the strap.

◆ With $3\frac{1}{2}$-inch common nails, join the 2-by-4s together in pairs, forming L-shaped braces.

◆ Working on a platform of plywood, position the braces against the inner sides of the strap ends and mark the bolt holes.

◆ Drill $\frac{1}{4}$-inch holes into the braces at each mark and secure the straps to the braces with $1\frac{1}{2}$-inch-long $\frac{3}{8}$-inch lag screws and washers (right).

8. Anchoring the braces.

◆ Bend each strap at a 45-degree angle by pivoting the brace and strap away from the chimney.

◆ Nail the braces to the joists to hold the straps in position, then drill a $\frac{3}{8}$-inch clearance hole through each brace where it crosses a joist. Stop drilling when the bit contacts the joist.

◆ With a $\frac{1}{4}$-inch bit, drill $1\frac{1}{2}$-inch-deep pilot holes into the joists at each contact point; then, fasten the braces with 3-inch-long $\frac{3}{8}$-inch lag screws and washers.

◆ Fill the gaps at the wall slots with exterior caulk.

Warding off Lightning Damage

Tall metal antennas on the roofs of houses are inviting targets for lightning, which seeks a path to the ground by the route that offers the least resistance. How much protection you need from the enormous destructive power of lightning depends on where you live.

Lightning Arresters: In general, all homes should at least have lightning arresters, or surge protectors, to safeguard household wiring and appliances from damage. Installed at the service panel and on television antenna lead-ins, these devices divert to ground electrical surges that would otherwise enter the house through overhead power and telephone lines or antenna cables from nearby lightning strikes. If you live in an area with frequent thunderstorms, or your home is isolated or is the tallest in the immediate vicinity, you should consider full-scale protection. In each case, installation calls for the expertise and special equipment of a lightning-protection professional.

Grounding a TV Antenna: One measure you can take is to ground your TV antenna mast *(below and page 122)*. You can ground other metal objects on the roof that go to ground, such as a stovepipe coming up from a wood stove, in the same way. Use ladders safely *(page 28)* and never work on the roof in windy or wet weather.

After installing a grounding cable, inspect it annually. Check for breaks or fraying, make certain that clamps and splices are tight, and verify that buried rods and cable are in good condition.

 TOOLS

Wire brush
Screwdriver
Putty knife
Maul
Shovel
Wrench
Lineman's
pliers

 **MATERIALS**

Unshielded
copper wire
(9-gauge)
Copper clips
with brass
screws
Grounding rod
Grounding
clamps
Sandpaper
(coarse grade)
Plastic roofing
cement

 **SAFETY TIPS**

Put on goggles while hammering in the rod.

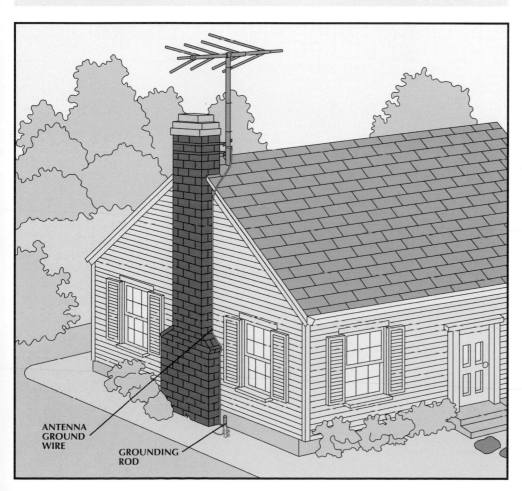

ANTENNA GROUND WIRE

GROUNDING ROD

Diverting lightning.
A television antenna is grounded by running a length of 9-gauge unshielded copper cable from the mast to a grounding rod buried underground; the rods are available in kits. As shown at left, the wire is clamped to the base of the antenna. Following the shortest path from the roof to the rod, the wire is fastened with clips to the house and clamped to the rod underground.

GROUNDING A TELEVISION ANTENNA

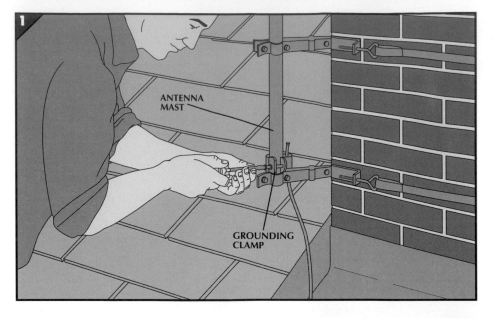

1. Connecting the cable to the antenna.

◆ Scrape any paint from the bottom few inches of the antenna mast with a wire brush, or sand it off, making sure to reach bare metal.

◆ Thread the cable through a grounding clamp, then tighten the clamp around the cable and the base of the antenna *(left)*.

2. Running the cable to the rod.

◆ Run the wire along the roof, fastening it every 3 feet with a copper clip and brass screw *(right)*; any bends should have a radius of at least 8 inches. To prevent roof leaks, dab plastic roofing cement over the screws with a putty knife.

◆ Continue running the cable down the wall, attaching it with clips. If it passes over a metal gutter, screw it to the gutter with a clip.

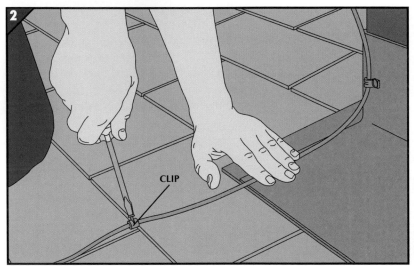

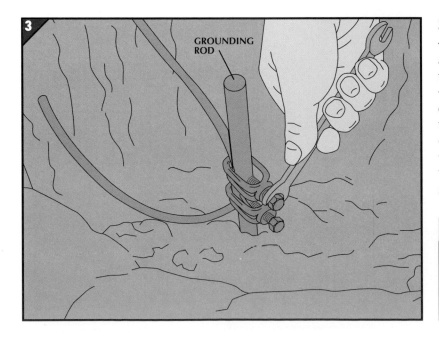

3. Connecting the cable to the rod.

◆ Dig a shallow hole next to the house; then, with a maul, drive the rod into the ground so at least 3 feet are buried.

◆ Slip a grounding clamp on the rod and slide it down to the base. Fit the grounding cable between the rod and the clamp, and tighten the clamp with a wrench *(left)*.

◆ Cut off the excess wire with lineman's pliers, then refill the hole to cover the top of the grounding rod.

⚠ CAUTION

Before driving a grounding rod, check for the location of underground utility lines exiting the house.

Coping with the Chaos of a Flood

When the threat of flood is imminent, there are several steps you can take to safeguard belongings and prepare for the disruption. Move as many valuables as possible to the second floor or attic. Store plastic jugs of water. Shut off electricity at the service panel and close the main water valve. Switch off the furnace, the water heater, and the valve for the oil tank, and unplug all appliances.

After the Flood: It can be dangerous to enter a house that has been flooded. The water may have caused structural or electrical damage. Animals may be trapped inside, and any mud left behind can contain harmful bacteria.

Reenter your home only after ascertaining that the foundation, walls, and electrical system are sound. If you have doubts, contact a contractor or inspector beforehand.

Draining the Basement: Pump out the basement slowly. As shown below, use a gas-powered trash pump, available at a tool rental center. Even if there is no standing water outside, saturated soil exerts tremendous force against the walls. If the water inside is removed quickly, the walls can cave in.

Any mud left behind should be removed quickly—it is usually easier to get rid of the mud before it dries and hardens. Shovel out as much as you can, then hose off all contaminated surfaces. Damaged wallboard will usually have to be removed *(page 125)*.

 TOOLS

	Shovel
	Hammer
Trash pump	Pry bar
Mop	Compass
Push broom	saw

SAFETY TIPS

Mud carried into a home by flooding can contain harmful bacteria, so always wear an antibacterial mask and rubber gloves when disposing of it. Wear safety goggles, a dust mask, gloves, and a long-sleeved shirt when demolishing walls or handling fiberglass insulation.

EXPELLING FLOODWATER

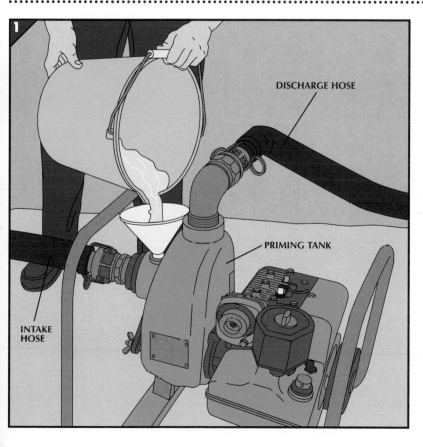

DISCHARGE HOSE

PRIMING TANK

INTAKE HOSE

1. Setting up a trash pump.
◆ Position the pump on level ground outside the house. Fit the intake hose onto the intake pipe and the discharge hose onto the discharge pipe, then tighten the clamps.
◆ Fill the priming tank with clean water *(left)* and secure the plug. Fill the tank with gasoline.

2. Pumping out the water.

◆ Position the discharge hose at a storm drain, then start the pump.

◆ Lower the intake hose through an open window *(right)* until the strainer is submerged.

◆ Pump out 2 to 3 feet of water and mark the water level. Check the level the next day. If it has risen, wait a day or two to empty the basement. Otherwise, pump out another 2 to 3 feet, repeating until the strainer has picked up as much water as possible.

STRAINER

3. Removing mud and debris.

◆ Remove the rest of the standing water with a mop, wringing it into a pail.

◆ With a push broom, push mud and debris into a pile; then, shovel it into a garbage can *(left)*.

◆ Rinse off the walls, ceilings, and floors with a garden hose. Mop up the floor again. Leave basement windows open so the basement can air out.

TRICKS OF THE TRADE

Pinpointing Gas Leaks

If natural gas pipes have been displaced by the flooding, brush soapy water on each connection. Any escaping gas will create bubbles. If you detect any leaks or smell gas, call your gas utility immediately.

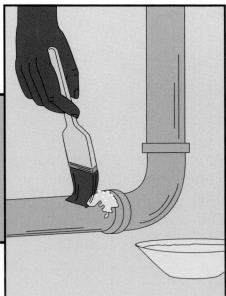

CLEANING AND DRYING WALLS

1. Breaking wet walls.
◆ Break away water-soaked wallboard or plaster with a hammer. Stop at the the mark left by the water.
◆ Remove any exposed nails with a pry bar.
◆ If the walls are insulated with rock wool or fiberglass, pull it out and discard it. For rigid polystyrene insulation, clean the surface with a hose.

BASEBOARD

SHOE MOLDING

2. Removing trim for cleaning.
◆ With a pry bar or putty knife, pry up and remove the shoe molding along the bottom of the walls.
◆ Partially pry the baseboard away from the studs (above), then release it to expose the nailheads holding it in place. Pull out the nails and carefully lift the baseboard out in sections.

3. Trimming walls.
◆ Wash the walls and framing with detergent.
◆ With a compass saw, trim the wallboard or plaster about 1 foot above the water line (left). Make sure the wall is completely dry before replacing the insulation and new wallboard.

INDEX

Time-Life Books is a division of Time Life Inc.

TIME LIFE INC.
PRESIDENT and CEO: George Artandi

TIME-LIFE BOOKS
PRESIDENT: John D. Hall
PUBLISHER/MANAGING EDITOR:
Neil Kagan

HOME REPAIR AND IMPROVEMENT:
Insulating and Weatherproofing
EDITOR: Lee Hassig
MARKETING DIRECTOR: James Gillespie
Deputy Editor: Esther R. Ferington
Art Director: Kathleen Mallow
Associate Editor/Research and Writing:
  Karen Sweet
Marketing Manager: Wells Spence

Vice President, Director of Finance:
  Christopher Hearing
Vice President, Book Production:
  Marjann Caldwell
Director of Operations: Eileen Bradley
Director of Photography and Research:
  John Conrad Weiser
Director of Editorial Administration:
  Judith W. Shanks
Production Manager: Marlene Zack
Quality Assurance Manager: James King
Library: Louise D. Forstall

ST. REMY MULTIMEDIA INC.
President and Chief Executive Officer:
  Fernand Lecoq
President and Chief Operating Officer:
  Pierre Léveillé
Vice President, Finance: Natalie Watanabe
Managing Editor: Carolyn Jackson
Managing Art Director: Diane Denoncourt
Production Manager: Michelle Turbide

Staff for Insulating and Weatherproofing

Series Editors: Marc Cassini, Heather Mills
Series Art Director: Francine Lemieux
Art Director: Robert Paquet
Assistant Editor: John Dowling
Designers: François Daxhelet,
  Jean-Guy Doiron, Robert Labelle
Editorial Assistant: James Piecowye
Coordinator: Dominique Gagné
Copy Editor: Judy Yelon
Indexer: Linda Cardella Cournoyer
Systems Coordinator: Éric Beaulieu
Other Staff: Lorraine Doré,
  Geneviève Monette

PICTURE CREDITS
Cover: Photograph, Glenn Moores and Chantal Lamarre. Art, Robert Paquet.

Illustrators: Gilles Beauchemin, Michel Blais, Adolph E. Brotman, Nick Fasciano, Michael Flanagan, Randall Lieu and Jim Silks, Peter McGinn, Jacques Perrault, Robert Ritter, John Sagan, Ray Skibinski, Vantage Art, Inc., Edward Vebell, Whitman Studio Inc.

Photographers: **End papers:** Glenn Moores and Chantal Lamarre. **8, 16, 25, 29, 33, 35, 56, 73, 75:** Glenn Moores and Chantal Lamarre. **15:** Kolbe & Kolbe Millwork Co., Inc. **63:** Mid-America Building Products. **69:** Brosz and Associates. **115:** Gulfstream Shutters Inc.

ACKNOWLEDGMENTS
The editors wish to thank the following individuals and institutions: Alumax Home Products, Lancaster, PA; Bon Tool Co., Gibsonia, PA; Brosz and Associates, Markham, Ont.; Cole Sewell Corporation, St. Paul, MN; Dow Chemical Canada Inc., Westmount, Que.; Eastern Awning Systems, Inc., Watertown, CN; Franklin International, Columbus, OH; Louis V. Genuario, Genuario Construction Company, Inc., Alexandria, VA; Gulfstream Shutters, Inc., Boca Raton, FL; Icynene Inc., Mississauga, Ont.; Industrial Fabrics Association International (Awning Division), St. Paul, MN; Kolbe & Kolbe Millwork Co., Inc., Wausau, WI; Marvin Windows & Doors, St. Paul, MN; McCoy Contractors, Milwaukee, WI; Mid-America Building Products, A Tapco International Company, Plymouth, MI; Midget Louver Co., Milford, CT; National Lightning Safety Institute, Louisville, CO; National Weather Service/National Hurricane Center, Miami, FL; Owens Corning, Toledo, OH; Pemko Manufacturing Company, Ventura, CA; Simpson Strong-Tie Company, Inc., Pleasanton, CA; 3M Do-It-Yourself and Construction Markets Division, St. Paul, MN; Water Ace Pump Company, Ashland, OH.

©1996 Time-Life Books. All rights reserved. No part of this book may be reproduced in any form or by any electronic or mechanical means, including information storage and retrieval devices or systems, without prior written permission from the publisher, except that brief passages may be quoted for reviews. First printing. Printed in U.S.A. Published simultaneously in Canada. School and library distribution by Time-Life Education, P.O. Box 85026, Richmond, Virginia 23285-5026.

TIME-LIFE is a trademark of Time Warner Inc. U.S.A.

Library of Congress
Cataloging-in-Publication Data
Insulating and weatherproofing / by the editors of Time-Life Books.
  p. cm. — (Home repair and improvement)
  ISBN 0-7835-3905-3
  1. Dwellings—Insulation—Amateurs' manuals. 2. Buildings—Airtightness—Amateurs' manuals. 3. Waterproofing—Amateurs' manuals.
  I. Time-Life Books. II. Series.
  TH1715.I627   1996
  693'.83—DC20   96-27521